Will You Come To Bed With Me?

Creating mindful moments with your family

Victoria Yuen

BALBOA.
PRESS

A DIVISION OF HAY HOUSE

"A refreshing read on creating a soulful family"

- Leonie Dawson.
Teacher, author, entrepreneur.

Balboa Press books may be ordered through booksellers or by contacting:

Balboa Press
A Division of Hay House
1663 Liberty Drive
Bloomington, IN 47403
www.balboapress.com.au
1 (877) 407-4847

Because of the dynamic nature of the Internet, any web addresses or
links contained in this book may have changed since publication and
may no longer be valid. The views expressed in this work are solely those
of the author and do not necessarily reflect the views of the publisher,
and the publisher hereby disclaims any responsibility for them.

The author of this book does not dispense medical advice or prescribe
the use of any technique as a form of treatment for physical, emotional,
or medical problems without the advice of a physician, either directly
or indirectly. The intent of the author is only to offer information
of a general nature to help you in your quest for emotional and
spiritual well-being. In the event you use any of the information in
this book for yourself, which is your constitutional right, the author
and the publisher assume no responsibility for your actions.

Any people depicted in stock imagery provided by Thinkstock are
models, and such images are being used for illustrative purposes only.
Certain stock imagery © Thinkstock.

Print information available on the last page.

ISBN: 978-1-4525-3082-6 (sc)
ISBN: 978-1-4525-3083-3 (e)

Balboa Press rev. date: 09/17/2015

CONTENTS

INTRODUCTION

Will you come to bed with me?

I can't tell you how many times I have heard this sentence.

I teach people to relax. It seems that the gift that has been given to me is to send people to sleep. After teaching a Yoga class and giving my yogis a lovely down-time session, one of the first things people say is… 'will you come to bed with me?'

I look at them sweetly and they suddenly realise what they have said, after they stop being all flustered, they tell me how much trouble they have falling asleep, or going back to sleep after waking at 3am, and they relax so easily with my voice.

I was once rung in the middle of the day by a stranger on the other side of the world who was suffering 3 days of jet lag, they had been told I could put them to sleep… yep, nighty nighty.

After teaching a Yoga class I would go home at night and my son would say 'will you come to bed with me?' We were still recovering from a very troublesome time since his birth, and we got into the habit of sleeping together, as he had to sleep upright, so I held onto him.

We all do what we have to do to get by, but times change and we don't have to hold onto these habits, unless they continue to be what's right for us at that particular moment. I have now taught him his own relaxation techniques, so he is comfortable sleeping by himself. He still has troubles waking up at night, and we are currently doing the exact techniques I am going to teach you, so you too can help your children. Here's hoping it will set him up for the rest of his life, just as it has with my eldest.

So, will YOU come to bed with me?

Will you come into a safe, lovely, relaxed place and let go of all of the day's tension and soften your body so that it drifts off into a peaceful dreamy place, giving you a full night's blissful rest?

Or will you stay up late having rushed home to scoff down your dinner, have a few wines pretending to relax while you watch gut wrenching news and checking your accounts on your phone while acting as if you are listening to your kids read and do their homework?

Will you come to bed with your laptop and check emails one last time before settling down to sleep with a tired, tight, stressed-out and sore body, already thinking about the next day and having everyone in your head, from your boss, to the hairdresser, to the kids teacher, chatting to you?

Will you have found a way to eat at least 3 hours before bed, stop drinking and screen time an hour before bed, have no electronic equipment in the bedroom to disturb your sleep patterns, have a darkened room, and (hopefully) everything in order for the next day so it's a peaceful morning?

Your body is relaxed and ready for sleep. The kids have done the same thing, because they will be following your lead, and they are already peacefully asleep, giving you and your partner some much needed cuddle time.

Is this laughable for you? Can I hear you gigglesnorting from here?

Let's sort this life out before we realise that each day has passed and it's exactly the same as the previous day, and suddenly you've had 20 years of crappy sleep deprived stressed days and nights, which turn into illness or disease, or already has.

Stress has been part of my everyday life for many years; I seem to be wired that way. You know those people that are all chilled and relaxed, you know, they sing in the shower and tell you to 'just get over it' when you're suffering depression?

Well, I'm NOT one of them, I'm jealous of them.

I'm the person that people tell me to;
'stop thinking so much,'
'stop analysing everything,'
'stop being stressed, you're making your baby worse.'

I had my first stress related operation when I was 10 months old, since then I have had so many, the specialist told me he can't operate anymore and I'll have to cope with it with morphine for the rest of my life. That was 7 years ago.

No-one ever bothered to tell me 'how' to stop thinking, or analysing or stressing. Except for now, I'm going to tell you, because I've learnt how to.

It wasn't an easy path for me and I want to help make it a little smoother for you. I'll teach you to recognise your stress and what to do with it. I won't be able to stop stressful situations coming up in your life, but I'll give you the tools so you can choose how to react to that stress and how to help your kids deal with this ever increasing manic world that we live in.

I have taught hundreds of people, from all walks of life, and I know with these simple proven techniques that we will learn together, you will be able to create a calmer, happier life.

So when my stomach specialist gave me that beautiful (not) piece of information, I had to have quite a bit of wine and it sent me into a dark place in my head for some time. I started to reassess ALL of my life at that stage. I realised that only I could change things if I wanted to. I can happily say that I haven't been back to hospital since that appointment.

I'm going to give you a number of techniques that I have researched, trialled, failed, tried again, tweaked and changed to fit into a busy parent's lifestyle.

So what is stress?

Life line tells us that 'stress is a natural human response to pressure when faced with challenging and sometimes dangerous situations. That pressure is not only about what's happening around us, but often also about demands we place on ourselves.'

When we have a stressful situation, our beautiful bodies try to protect us.

This comes from when we had to run away from rhinos that might want to eat us.

Our body fills with gorgeous adrenaline, so that we can run really, really fast or fight. It reminds me of those stories that you hear of when people get superhuman strength and can lift a heavy object off a person's trapped body, ever hear of a story like that?

It's amazing what our bodies can do.

The trouble is that in our normal, everyday life, we don't have to run from rhinos, and hopefully we don't have to save anyone regularly, but our bodies haven't really cottoned on to that. The same response, the fight or flight response, happens in our bodies when we feel we are in a stressful situation.

And unfortunately, the latest research is now saying, we don't even have to be physically in the situation, we can get the same flight or fight response just THINKING about that situation.

So where does that leave us? In a good stressful situation, such as a wedding, or a sporting game, starting something exciting you haven't tried before, stress can be good! It increases our ability to be alert, energised, switched on and resourceful. But unfortunately stress plays more of a role in the unpleasant side of our lives, it leaves us feeling tired, tense, anxious, burnt out or overwhelmed, which leads to trouble sleeping.

Without putting too much of a dampener on things, stress has been associated with obesity, heart disease, Alzheimer's disease, diabetes, cancer, depression, sleep disorders, gastrointestinal problems, and asthma.

Ok, before we get all stressed out about being stressed, this is why we are here, so we can nip this in the bud and take as much stress OUT of our lives and create that long lasting health and happiness we deserve.

Take a deep breath.

So we know that we don't want stress in our lives, but how do we do this?

When my son was born, he was quite unwell, and screamed and vomited so much that he ripped the lining of his stomach and throat so he vomited blood, and as a Mum, you know you want to do everything you can to help your child, so you can imagine I was a very worried. At his 6 week check-up, the doctor asked my Mum to take him from the room, because my son screamed so much we couldn't hear each other, and the doctor said that me being stressed, might be causing him to be worse and I needed to stop being stressed.

Now the doctor wasn't the first person to say this to me, no one told me 'how' not to be stressed and the doctor just handed me an antidepressant script.

So I'm going to give YOU some tips.

Firstly you need to recognise your personal signs of stress in your body, for me, my belly swells so much it looks like I'm 6 months pregnant and my memory goes whack.

Yours could be memory problems, inability to concentrate, poor judgment, seeing only the negative, anxious or racing thoughts, constant worrying, moodiness, irritability or short temper, agitation, inability to relax, feeling overwhelmed, sense of loneliness and isolation, depression or general unhappiness, aches and pains, diarrhoea or constipation, nausea, dizziness, chest pain, rapid heartbeat, loss of sex drive, frequent colds, eating more or less, sleeping too much or too little, isolating yourself from others, procrastinating or neglecting responsibilities, using alcohol, cigarettes, or drugs to relax, nervous habits (e.g. nail biting, pacing). Ref: http://www.helpguide.org/

Keep in mind that the signs and symptoms of stress can also be caused by other psychological or medical problems. If you're experiencing any of the warning signs of stress, it's important to see a doctor for a full evaluation. Your doctor can help you determine whether or not your symptoms are stress-related. Ask around for a doctor that really listens to you. One that you feel comfortable with and resonates with your way of life.

There is a really great quiz on this website. <u>http://www.</u>
<u>helpguide.org/articles/stress/stress-symptomscauses-and-</u>
<u>effects.htm</u>

OK, so now we know what stress is, how it affects our bodies and can see how it affects us personally, let's find out what we can do about it, so we can sleep well.

The first and MOST important technique that I would like you to take away from this book is a simple one.
I'm going to teach you how to breathe properly.
What's so good about breathing?
Most of us don't breathe properly, which means we aren't getting enough oxygen into our bodies and minds. We need oxygen in our bodies to help us make clear decisions and so our muscles get the nutrients to keep us going.

All of the techniques that I teach you in this book, will need you to breathe properly, with your diaphragm muscle. Use this correct way of breathing, not just sometimes, but training yourself to breathe this way all the time. This is the way babies breathe, why? Because babies are incredibly clever. At some stage along our lives, we stuff things up, store bad emotions and habits in our nervous system and stop breathing properly.

Let's have a go….

Firstly stop and listen to your breath, with no emotion or judgment, acknowledge where the breath is going, is it going into the top part of the lungs, or the lower part of the lungs?

You may want to close your eyes, but visualise your breath going all the way down into the bottom parts of your lungs as you breathe in. When the breath enters the bottom part of the lungs, your belly will rise slightly. When you breathe out gently from the bottom of your lungs, your belly with contract. Do a couple of gentle rounds of this breathing, see if you can soften your shoulders and soften the muscles in your face. OK, now stop thinking about the breath and continue normally. Place one hand on your belly and one hand on your chest, you should be able to see the hand on your belly move slightly out when you breathe IN and slightly in as you breathe OUT.

Just relax and try this for a few more rounds.

This is called diaphragmatic breathing or belly breathing. Yogis call breath control Pranayama.

As we move the air to the bottom part of our lungs the diaphragm muscle moves down, gently pushing and massaging our internal organs and expanding the belly. When we breath out the diaphragm muscle pushes the lungs up to help release the air and contracts and strengthens our abdominal muscles.

What a perfect combination our bodies give us every single time we breath properly.

A massage for your internal system and a gentle abdominal workout with every breath.

CHAPTER 1

Sleep

I'm a sleep slut.
I can do it anywhere,
anytime with anyone.

Did you know that sleep deprivation used to be a torture technique?

Anyone who has had babies will understand exactly what I'm saying. Imagine living in that sleep deprived way for years and years, instead of months.

I am certain that is why there are those signs on the back of people's cars, "Baby On Board", because when you see that, you know to keep WAY clear, that person is sleep deprived and won't have their full brain functioning.

I can sort of understand, just a little, as I stop breathing every 3 minutes when I'm asleep, which according to the doctors, really isn't that bad as sleep apnoea goes. I have it sorted now, but it has taken years off my life and I went down the destructive track of finding hard stimulants to keep me awake.

Unfortunately stress is the number one cause of short-term sleeping difficulties, according to sleep experts.

Our jobs, families, money worries or illness put constant pressure on us and affect our sleep patterns.

Hopefully when these certain problems have passed, we can go back to our normal sleep routine, but sometimes long-lasting insomnia occurs.

So what's important about getting a great sleep?

A good night's rest will help our bodies and minds rejuvenate. Sleep will keep your immune system healthy and will help you regulate your moods.

So how much sleep do YOU actually need?

Everybody is different and here's a chart to help you, but I think we need to keep in mind that it's the quality of sleep we are getting that's important.

Newborns
16–18 hours a day
Preschool-aged children
11–12 hours a day
School-aged children
At least 10 hours a day
Teens
9–10 hours a day

Adults ((including the elderly)
7–8 hours a day

This might help you understand sleep needs to be a BIG priority in your life;

- It is stated that 60-80% of patients with depression report experiencing sleep disturbances of some kind.

- According to the NHSA, falling asleep while driving is responsible for at least 100,000 crashes, 71,000 injuries and 1,550 deaths each year in the United States. Young people in their teens and twenties, who are particularly susceptible to the effects of chronic sleep loss, are involved in more than half of the fall-asleep crashes each year.

- With insufficient sleep you will have trouble making decisions, solving problems, controlling your emotions and behaviour, and coping with change.

- When you are asleep your body can heal and repair your heart and blood vessels. Ongoing sleep deficiency is linked to an increased risk of heart disease, kidney disease, high blood pressure, diabetes, and stroke.

- A good night's sleep can keep you in a good weight range. Not only will you have enough energy to exercise during the day, sleep helps maintain a healthy balance of the hormones that make you feel hungry (ghrelin) or full (leptin). When you don't get enough sleep, your level of ghrelin goes up and

your level of leptin goes down. This makes you feel hungrier than when you're well-rested.
Ref: http://www.nhlbi.nih.gov

- Sleep also affects how your body reacts to insulin, the hormone that controls your blood glucose (sugar) level. Sleep deficiency results in a higher than normal blood sugar level, which may increase your risk for diabetes.

    In order to get a good night's sleep, preparation and routine is the key. As always, the process begins with YOU. You need to acknowledge that sleep is integral to stress management and make sleep a priority over other activities.

We know that not every night will have the same in store for us. We will have situations that come up, a party, a late night meeting, a long phone call to a friend, kids being sick and needing attention, a new-born, but if we can see that this isn't the norm, and make the majority of our nights similar, it will benefit you in enormous ways, physically and mentally.

Here are some tips of preparing yourself for some lovely zzzzz's, then we'll get to tips to help you get back to sleep at the dreaded 3am 'racing monkey-mind' wake up time. (If you are one of the hundreds of people that I hear say "I just can't stop my thoughts" check out the technique in Chapter 7 on how to de-clutter your mind.)

Keep alcoholic bevies limited and grab your last cup of caffeine no later than 2 in the afternoon.

Limit your really hard core workouts to day time sessions and use slow restorative Yoga to stretch and slow the body down in the evening.

The same with your mental hard core training, keep it to day time. I read prolifically, and I always keep my neuroscience books for the day, and my romantic or funny fluff for night time.

Try to keep a similar waking and sleeping time each day, including the weekends.

Have a dark room to help your amazing eyes send a signal to your amazing brain to process the sleep chemicals (melatonin). The signal will then be sent to your amazing body, and tells your body it's time to go nigh-nighs, clever hey?

Napping during the day will disrupt your sleep patterns, so if you're like me and think that taking a nap in the day is one of the best things in the world, here's a little trick that I use.

Legs up the wall.

You sit sideways against a wall, with your hip up on the skirting board. Then gently twist your body so that you lay down on your back and bring your legs up the wall. We call this position, Inverted Lake pose.

5 minutes in this position is said to be equivalent to 20 minutes deep rest and 20 minutes is equivalent to an hour.

I like to put on a guided meditation using ear buds when I do this pose. If you have tight hammies, then either bend the knees or bring the soles of the feet together and relax the knees out to the side.

It's important for adults and children to have a screen free hour before they go to bed. The light from the types of screens we have currently stimulate brain functions, great for day time, not so great for night time.

An hour may seem a long time for some, but let's have a think about it, once you've all eaten dinner together and had no screen, as we all know that a dinner table conversation is one of the base keys to keep open communication in the household, then it's clean-up, then it's shower/bath time for kids, then it it's dressing and stories, either them reading to you, or you reading to them, or them reading by themselves.

By now, it's probably over an hour. You and the kids have had quality time together, everyone's chilled and ready for bed and you've all set yourself up for an awesome sleep.

I suggest, that if you use the 'time-out' technique for disciplining little kids, don't use the bedroom, find another area in your house. My kids had to sit in the laundry with the door open, nothing to play with and really boring.

So what's to stop you, as an adult, doing the same routine as the kids? (The sleep prep, not the 'time-out'! Although I can remember many times that all I wanted was some time-out when it was crazy time in my house.)

How about a relaxing bath, a good book or audio book if you're not a reader, splendid!

The way you feel while you're awake depends in part on what happens while you're sleeping.

During sleep, your body is working to support healthy brain functioning and maintain your physical health. In children and teens, sleep also helps support growth and development.

Remember the diaphragmatic breathing we practised in the Introduction? This is the way we need to breathe every time we do a breathing exercise and it will be the basis of all of the following techniques.

If it makes you feel uncomfortable, just practise a few rounds and each time increase the number of repetitions. With regular practise you will see it gets really easy, very quickly and you will find yourself doing the proper breathing technique without even trying.

These techniques are great to do when you get into bed or when you wake and can't get back to sleep. They are also good to be done around your children, so you can mentor them in a positive way. When I first started doing this around my kids, I said out loud what I'm doing.

Yogis call these types of practises 'Pratyahara', which means 'going within.'

The techniques are easy enough for parents and children. I like to teach methods that you can do anywhere and you don't have to buy fancy equipment.

Technique 1. Quick release.

Take a deep breath in through the nose and out through the mouth, do this 3 times and then focus on your normal breath.

Try to remember this breathing technique next time you feel your stress triggers coming up, you will still have to deal with the stress, but hopefully it won't affect you as much because you're coming at it from a calmer place. Simple hey?

Technique 2. Counting breath.

Rest comfortably, place one hand on your belly and one hand on your chest, relax your shoulders and allow your elbows to be heavy. Count how many seconds it takes for you to breathe in and how many seconds it takes for you to breathe out.

Just watch and listen and count for about 30 seconds.

Now try to make the breaths the same length, do for about 30 seconds.

Lengthen the inhale and the exhale by one second.

Do for about 30 seconds. Then increase it again by another second on the inhale and exhale and do for about 30 seconds, or more if you feel comfortable.

Just ease into it and continue to count the breath, or let go of the controlled breathing and fall into a lovely relaxed sleep.

Technique 3. Tense and Release

Relax for 30 seconds and soften into your body using the belly breathing technique.

Squeeze your toes together and hold them tight for 20 seconds and release. Feel the difference between tense and relaxed.

Pushing your heels into the bed/floor, flex your feet and pull your toes towards your knees for 20 seconds and release.

*Tighten all of the muscles in your legs, pushing them down into the bed, **remember to breathe**, and relax. Spend a couple of moments feeling how nice it is to have relaxed legs.*

Pull in your stomach as hard as you can and feel how much this tightens your lungs and contracts your breathing.

Release and notice how nice it is not holding onto the pressure around your belly. Push your shoulders down into the bed, now your elbows, now your hands, hold for 20 seconds and release.

Feel the softening across your chest, feel the breath come gently in and out of your lungs, feel your shoulders start to melt and become heavy.

Now squish your face up as tight as you can, really squeeze your lips together, clench your jaw, tighten your eyes and frown as much as you can. Hold for an uncomfortable 30 seconds, and relax. Now take 3 deep breaths and relax some more, feel the muscles around your eyes relax, separate your teeth slightly and feel where your tongue is most comfortable. Feel the soft breath enter and exit your nose, relax some more around your eyes and your forehead.

Soften into sleep.

Technique 4. Body Scan.

Do a minute of full diaphragmatic breathing.

Relax the breath and soften the body.

Bring your attention inside your body.

As you think of each part of your body, try to relax and soften it. Just notice if there's any tension in one area of your body and without emotion or making a story about it, just release it and let it go.

Start either with the head or the feet.

If your attention wanders, gently bring your awareness back to the body scan.

Really feel each part of the body, for example, if you are starting at your feet; feel the pressure of the blanket or feel the air on your feet, feel the tips of the toes, feel each individual toe, feel the heel of the foot, feel the arch of the foot, feel the top of the foot, feel the inside of the foot.

Download a free guided meditation here: http://www. victoriasplaceonline.com.au/?p=1966

Technique 5. Mindfulness breathing.

Do a minute of full diaphragmatic breathing.

Relax the breath and start to just watch the thoughts pass on through your head.

Observe them as events in your life, try not to let them take over your whole mind and don't make a story about them, just noticing for about a minute.

Start listening to your breath again, on an inhale count 1, on an exhale count 2, inhale count 3, exhale count 4 and so on until you get to 10, then start again.

When people start this practise, they can usually get to 4 and then the thoughts start wandering in again, that's OK, gently bring them back to counting the breath. Continue until you are relaxed and asleep.

There are 5 relaxation techniques that don't require any equipment, you can do them anywhere.

A friend of mine came to me on Friday night and thanked me for teaching her this, because her tweenage daughter was having a melt down and she encouraged her to do the counting breath, and tadah, only a tiny melt down, not a full blown one, yippee!

Simple as the practises are that I'm going to give you, it's just like having a gym membership, if you don't do it, it's not going to help you.

CHAPTER 2

Mindful moments

I hate it when the voices in my head go quiet, I never know what they are planning. Anon

So moving onto your mind my lovely.

I remember going to a meditation retreat and the teacher asking me how I went. I smiled radiantly up at her and said;

'that was wonderful, I only had one conversation going on in my head, not heaps!'

I'm sure you can relate to this.

Usually we go through our day, not even enjoying what is in front of us, but having a conversation with someone from the past in our heads, or our thoughts are in the future worrying about what might or might not happen.

One thing I have learnt, is most of my concerns or worries that caused my unhappiness and stress, I actually make up myself.

I remember hanging out the washing and having a HUGE argument with someone in my head, it was making my heart race, my body was all tight and shaky, I felt sick, and I stopped and finally got it.

That person had NO idea they were yelling at me inside my head and I was yelling back.

I was causing my own stress.

The argument that started it, actually did happen, but it was also finished. I was the one continuing it and I was the one making myself sick, there was no one else hanging out the washing with me, it was my choice.

Now I'm not saying that stressful situations are always your choice, but that particular one of mine was.

So I want to talk to you about who's in your head and how to stop stressing.

Let's pretend you're getting into the shower.
Your kids are old enough that they have
stopped coming in with you and you're alone.
The water's warm, not a care in the world.
Then you start thinking about your upcoming day.
Your boss comes into the shower with you and chats to you about a deadline or something you missed.

Then you think about what you're going to wear that day and Trinny and Susannah come into the shower telling you which knickers will look good under that skirt.

Then you wonder whether the kids have clean clothes to wear to school and the kids come into the shower with you, then you wonder what you're having for dinner and it's getting ridiculously crowded, but you tell the butcher he can come into in too.

Are you still enjoying your shower?

Did you even realise you got out and you're drying yourself?

Did you remember to rinse the shampoo out?

Who would know, because everyone else was talking at the same time and you couldn't think…

but who was actually, physically there?

You, you were physically there, but you weren't there mentally.

This situation can happen all day.

We can live in the past or the future all day.

We get to the end of the day and can't actually remember what we did, because we were never really fully present and there.

We get to the end of the year and we say 'where did that year go?', well… it was actually there, but you weren't. How many years do we have to do this before we realise what we are missing?

Let's think about the shower and your health and happiness again.

You get into the shower, it's warm and delicious, you feel the water run from the crown of your head all the way to your toes, washing any tension from your shoulders, any concerns from your mind and any knots or butterflies from your belly. You pour the shampoo into your hand and look at the colour and smell the aroma. You shampoo your head using your fingers to massage your scalp, releasing any tension from your face and neck. You wash your body, remembering to check your boobs. Once you've finished you come out refreshed, calm and ready for the day.

So, like I said before, some stressful situations are out of our hands, but maybe we can work at the ones that we can change, like having a peaceful shower.

And with the ones that we can't change, let's try to look at our reactions to the situation.

To do this we need to train our minds to come into the present moment, often, and calm our thoughts. It's said that thinking too much about the past may cause depressive thoughts and worrying too much about the future may cause anxious thoughts.

I'm going to give you a great technique, to 1) be present and 2) train your mind.

Firstly a little about your mind.

I have been avidly following the latest research on neuroplasticity, which makes me kinda dull, but it floats my boat at the moment, because it's having such a huge impact on health and happiness.

Very quickly, neuroplasticity is the science behind how we can adapt our brains and re-wire them. We can physically re-train our own minds.

Very, very simply put, if someone told us that we were, shall we say 'dumb at maths', and our minds then decided that because we were 'dumb at maths' we would stop trying, our neural pathways in this area would actually become weaker.

But if we turned it around later in life and thought to ourselves; 'maybe I'm not dumb at maths, maybe that person was just having a bad day and taking it out on me, this isn't something that I needed to hold onto for the past 34 years,' then started training the brain muscle, we can re-wire the brain to create thicker neural pathways and we can actually make ourselves better, amazing right?

The only problem is, the same with the muscles in your bodies, the brain muscle requires constant attention to continue to develop.

So make it fun, just as it's easier to enjoy exercise when it's fun, it's easier to re-wire your brain when it's fun.

I don't do triathlons, because that's not fun for my body and I don't do crosswords, because that's not fun for my mind, but good friends of mine love doing both.

I like to do Yoga because that's fun for my body and I like to listen to the latest TED talks on neuroplasticity, because that's fun for my mind.

So what's this all got to do with creating calm and relaxation in your household?

You now have the knowledge that YOU can change your own thoughts. Just because someone told you something negative in the past, it doesn't mean you still have to hold onto it, stopping your chance to create your own happiness and letting it affect your health.

Let's just say that again, you can say it with me if you want.

Just because someone told me something negative in the past, it doesn't mean I still have to hold onto it, stopping my chance to create my own happiness and letting it affect my health.

How does that make you feel?

Let's take a deep breath. If you have something that came up just then, here's your chance to let it go now, breathe it out.

You are in charge baby, you're the boss! What do YOU want out of your life?

Through changing your thought patterns, basically the sky's the limit, unless you want to be an astronaut, then the sky's not even the limit for you!

The first thing we need to do to change our thought patterns is to recognise what our thoughts are actually saying.

One easy way to do this is to put the thoughts into 3 categories.

Thoughts from the past, the present and the future.

For example; past thoughts could be remembering a conversation or something that has already happened. Present thoughts could be thinking about how hungry you are or thinking about how itchy the side of your head is. Future thoughts are thinking about something that hasn't happened yet.

All of these thoughts are useful for us, we need to remember the past, we need recognise we are hungry, we need to prepare for the future, but perhaps not all at the same time.

Yogis call meditation Dhyana.

Here are some great techniques for you, they are awesome for all ages.

Technique 1.

We are going to do another technique that will be easy for you to do anytime, anywhere.

If you feel as though your mind is racing, do a breathing technique that we have practised and then start listening to your thoughts. This can be one of the ways to start detaching yourself from negative thought patterns. It allows the thoughts to pass through you instead of making you worry. The thought could then be replaced with happier or neutral one.

Do not pursue these thoughts, judge them or reject them. Simply acknowledge them, and let them go. Ask yourself if it was a past, present or future thought and imagine that thought being placed into either a past, present or future box.

Pop the book down, and give it a go.

Here is your link to the downloadable meditation: http://www.victoriasplaceonline.com.au/?p=1893

Technique 2.

Do one of the breathing techniques that suit you to chillax for at least 2 minutes.

Bring your inner gaze to the space just behind the middle of the eye-brows, and watch what you see. It may be colours, patterns, or nothing at all. Anything you see here is normal.

When you have finished watching the colours and your thoughts start to creep into your mind, imagine you are tiny, and you are sitting just behind your eyebrows, on the inside of your skull, looking into your brain. I want you to start watching your thoughts float around your brain. See what colours they are, allow your thoughts to float around and then dissolve.

Stay there until you are ready to come out of your mind.

This technique reminds us that we can watch our thoughts.

Our thoughts are just words going around in your head, they don't have to affect us physically or emotionally.

For the kiddlets:

This is a similar technique to the previous one, just a little bit more picturesque.

You can download this meditation here: http://www.victoriasplaceonline.com.au/?p=1968

The children find a relaxing breathing technique that they enjoy and start to relax their bodies. Once they are soft and relaxed, we remind them that to be aware of their breathing, and they will continue breathing. Imagine they are under water, floating at the bottom of a pond. Looking up they can see the sunlight rippling across the surface, (remind them again that it's a special pond and they can still breathe easily). They see their first fish floating past, let them know that it's a happy fish. Ask them to think about what colour it is, (they can answer aloud or mentally,) what size it is, how it moves and allow the first fish to float away. The next fish they see is an angry fish, ask them the same questions. Continue with this process, using different emotions, whatever you think your children need at their age and during whatever they are going through. Only use about 6 or 7 fish, the last fish, should be their choice, ask them how that fish is feeling? What colour is it? How does it move? Where is it going? When you feel your child is ready, allow them to relax on their side for a few moments and then, if they want to, have a chat about their last fish and how they felt about watching all the other fish.

Technique 3.

When you have finished doing your favourite relaxation breathing technique, imagine that you are sitting inside and looking out the window at a street. As thoughts come into your mind, visualise they are cars and watch them pass on by, out of your eye-sight, without giving them any more attention.

Technique 4.

When you have finished doing your favourite relaxation breathing technique, imagine you are a cat. You are watching a mouse hole. Each time you see a mouse scamper across the mouse hole, imagine this was a thought, and it's running away.

Technique 5.

I'd hate to be biased, but the next technique I'm going to teach you was the most powerful one for me in improving my health and happiness.

This next tip involves stepping out of your ego and really listening to what is going on in your mind and seeing how it physically affects your body.

We spoke previously about having other people inside your head. Some voices are really loud, but others can be very subtle. I gave you an example of someone saying you were 'dumb at maths' so you stopped trying and are still believing them 34 years later.

Let's think about something a little more sensitive. Perhaps someone said something about your weight, or you were totally obsessed with looking at the skinny models in magazines thinking you should be this way to be happy. You might not even remember it, but this will stick with you, and without making a true commitment to be happy with your weight, you will probably always struggle with self-love.

A quick story for you.

When I was a school teacher, I was totally dedicated to doing the best job I could and helping the kids in my classes thrive. I used to speak to the professionals e.g psychiatrists, speech pathologists, etc in my spare time to see what else I could do to be a better teacher. I was speaking to a nurse one afternoon and asking for some more ideas on how to help a particular lad with his autistic tendencies, and she said "would you stop butting in on other people's jobs and just focus on your own for once."

So I found someone else to talk to.

A couple of years later I had to take one of my babies to see her so they could get their immunisations, I was terrified. Unfortunately she remembered me and we just focussed solely on my child. Just as we were leaving, she pulled me aside, and said with a beetroot red face, "Look Victoria, I just wanted to say sorry if I said anything sharp to you when you were a teacher. I have suffered the most debilitating headaches for years and I have only just found some relief for them, and I realised this may have affected my communications with people." I thanked her and wished her good health from now on.

Perhaps we can remember that if someone has said something negative towards to us in the past, it may not solely be about us, and this is what I mean about having to get out of your ego.

It may not all be about us, everyone has their issues.

We don't need to accept negativity into our lives, and most importantly, we need to recognise that the negativity is affecting our own health and happiness, and it is our own choice whether to take this into our cells, or not.

Next time a negative thought pattern comes into your mind, take some time to

1) *recognise it,*
2) *see if you can detach your emotion from it*
3) *have a little thought, without judgement, about where it may have come from*
4) *let it go or perhaps replace it with a neutral or positive thought.*

CHAPTER 3

———— ❖ ————

Fighting the battle of food

Q: Why don't eggs tell jokes?
A: They'd crack each other up!

I hate it when I think I'm buying
organic vegetables and they end
up being regular old donuts.

This has been an incredibly hard chapter for me to write, because up until recently I hated food.

Food for me meant pain, sometimes when I ate certain foods, it caused my stomach to contract, swell and I'd either vomit or have diarrhoea or both at the same time. These situations happened in my life so frequently, they seemed to cover up all of the other times when it wasn't so bad, which I think was probably most of the time.

After all of my stomach operations, surely one of the doctors/specialists/gastroenterologist should have mentioned that I should really look into the foods that I am eating and that maybe, just maybe, something that I was eating wasn't agreeing with me?

It seems pretty obvious now.

My body is different from your body. Your body is different from your sister's, your mother's, your cousin's.

Your body is even different from the body that you were born with, your taste buds have changed, your skin has grown, you can tolerate more than milk.

We need to be very receptive to what our OWN body needs. Take advice from the specialists and give things a try if they seem safe for you. Do the research, but only do what is good for your OWN body.

Just because I feel better eating a wheat/gluten free diet, doesn't mean that it will be the best for you. Just because your mate is doing a completely raw food diet and she is telling everyone how much energy she has, doesn't mean that it will suit your body type.

I personally found that the more Yoga I did, the more I got to know the subtle nuances of my own body, therefore I could start to manage what I put into my body. Don't get me wrong, I'm not good ALL of the time, but this is my choice. I understand that I will suffer the consequences, and sometimes the chocolate cake is worth it!

Just like everything else, balance and fun is the key, or you won't stick to it. It won't become a lifestyle.

Two things I very much recommend, whole foods and mindful eating.

As much as you possibly can, eat whole seasonal local foods.

Whole foods meaning foods that can be grown, not chemically put together. Try to keep away from any foods that have numbers in them.

Numbers are for accountants, not your precious tummy. Remind yourself there are nearly as many neurones in your tummy as there are in your brain.

We have talked how important it is to keep your brain healthy, well, your tummy is your emotional brain. Ever noticed when you're in a mood you crave certain foods? This is your emotional mind triggering you. YOU have the choice about what to put inside your body, you are not a child anymore, you have the choice.

Eat seasonally as much as you can.

Oranges grow well when our bodies need more vitamin C in the winter, clever Mother Earth. Our natural environment suits how we should live, keep it as natural as you can.

A lot of the foods we buy in the shops travel so far, we need to give some thought about the process.

Planting and growing your food; what chemicals are put into the soil and on the foods to make them grow?

Have they been genetically modified to grow fatter and quicker?

Storage; where are they stored, have they been washed first? How long are they stored for?

Processing; what is put into the foods to make them last longer on the shelves and to look nicer? Are they completely changed into a different product and what is the process of this?

Packaging; Where does the packaging come from? How clean is it? Does it come from a country with the same packaging laws as us?

Sales; How long has it been on the shelf, how many people and who have been touching the product?

Consumption; are you eating the product the way that it should be eaten or are you cooking it so that all of the (what's left) nutrients are being cooked out? Things have become so bad that some countries send their products overseas to get washed/processed/packaged by cheaper labour and then sent back here, making the time-line from farm to supermarket so much longer.

Product of Australia? Yes, but how far did it have to travel in order to be in our supermarkets? There's even a 'new' movement now called 'From Farm To Plate' or 'Farm To Fork'. The premise is; let's pick it from the garden and cook it and eat it. Well derrr, isn't this how it's always meant to be?

I have always had a veggie patch. I'm not very good at it, but I like my basil fresh, and it's great to have veggies all the time. I have recently moved to a place with no dirt, just bricks, so everything is in pots now, it works really well. Ideally I'll overcome my fear of scary chooks and get a chook pen for my eggs also, but I will have to wait till I get some yummy dirt for them to scratch around in.

So now we have the food part sorted for you, what's the mindful part got to do with anything?

Ever get to the end of a meal and not remember eating it?

Ever spend hours preparing a gorgeous meal and watched everyone scoff it down while watching TV not even thinking about how much effort you have put into the food?

Well, it's all about to change my lovely.

Mindful eating will help you in so many ways.

Firstly it's a great way to loose or maintain a healthy weight. When you are fully in the present moment and eating, you REALLY enjoy your food (I'll give you an example of this soon), and you will start to learn to listen to the indicators that your body is sending you saying that it's full. If you are sitting in front of the TV or computer, you aren't focused on your eating and you can miss these 'I'm full now, don't feed me anymore' signals that our body is giving us and we may eat too much.

Here's a way to really enjoy your food; mindful eating.

It's a family game, so get everyone involved.

Turn off the TV, sit at the table together. Start by thanking the person who has prepared the meal, feeling grateful for their time and effort and giving some thought about where the food has come from and the other people who have taken the time and effort into preparing your meal e.g. the farmers, shop keepers, packers, truck drivers etc.

Smell the food. Look at the food. Taste the food. Feel how the food feels in your mouth without speaking. Take some time between mouthfuls to feel what it feels like to have the lingering tastes in the mouth without the foods. You may even want to spend this time chatting with your family?

You'll probably find that they are quite interesting, and they may find YOU quite interesting!

When you are finished, have a moment before running away to let the food digest and for you to feel the joy of a full belly, it is a privilege denied to many. That food now is going to be shared throughout your body to your internal organs, your brain, your muscles, your blood. Now you know you have given your body the best food you can in order for it to work well for YOU.

When we are mindfully eating, we can recognise our emotional cues for food and we can choose whether we want to fulfil them or perhaps think about another way to fulfil this emotional need, say a walk around the block or a power nap?

Maybe your body is confusing hunger and thirst?

Our body is mainly made up of water, if we don't keep this at an equal balance, all sorts of nasty pasty things start to happen.

You may want to start thinking mindfully about why you eat.

Do you eat because it's the right time of day and that's what you have always done as a child? Are you eating because you're bored?

Because there was a great advertisement and the marketer has done such an amazing job you're actually salivating?

Also thinking about after you have eaten.

Every food has an energy level, are you using that energy that you have put into your body or are you letting it sit around your waist/hips/thighs/ arteries?

Please don't judge yourself too harshly here, food and weight can be a very emotive issue.

As I said before, once we learn how OUR particular body reacts to foods and learn what to do with the energy that we can harness, then everything starts to come together like magic.

Just start with being mindful. Part of the Yogic philosophy are the Yamas. These are the moral, ethical and societal guidelines for a practicing yogi. One of the five Yamas is Ahimsa, which translates to non-harming. When we bring this into the scope of food and our own bodies, we find ourselves looking at each thing that we place in our mouth and asking ourselves, is this non-harming for my body? Am I being compassionate to my internal organs, my blood system and with this food I put into my mouth, am I giving my brain the nourishment it needs? You may like to try this next time you eat.

CHAPTER 4

Get your groove on

You want to change something?
Sure! I'm a Yogini.
I'm flexible in my mind and body.
Victoria Yuen

I joined a health club last year; spent
about 400 bucks. Haven't lost a pound.
Apparently you have to show up. Anon

Your fitness routine will have to change during your lifetime, our bodies change, our routines change, our family circumstances change. It is important to find something that you like. You're not going to stick with it if you don't. Fitness needs to be part of your everyday, it doesn't have to be the same everyday, but build SOMETHING into it.

You would have to be living under a rock not to know that exercise is good for your health and happiness, and as a Yoga teacher, I can't recommend it enough. But, I understand that Yoga isn't for everyone, out of the hundreds of people I have taught, 3 haven't liked it, all good, no problem. Find something that you do like.

During my training for Encore, an exercise program for post surgery breast cancer, they said 'when exercising you should be just able to speak, but not able to sing.' Your heart beat needs to be raised. If you are completely bed ridden, there are always stretches that can be done. Try for 30 minutes a day, and as we are all busy, this may have to be split up into smaller chunks.

I truly believe as I mentioned previously, that you need to enjoy it.

If you don't know what you enjoy, try everything, just raise that gorgeous heart rate of yours.

Swimming, walking, running, Zumba, pole dancing, hopscotch, sex (and not the lie on your back and think of England type), boot camp, hockey practice with the kids, dancing.

At the moment, apart from Ashtanga Yoga, but favourite is exercise is kayaking, then I get to bob about in the water when I stop, it's so peaceful.

Since the weather has turned though, I have been putting 'Just Dance' on the Wii and getting my groove on with my kids laughing at me, good fun for the whole family!

Exercise can be a form of meditation. A very good girlfriend of mine swims for miles, she finds this incredibly relaxing and cathartic.

Me?

I flap about looking like a washing machine when I get in the water, certainly not relaxing, to do or watch! We are all different and that is OK. What your gorgeous friend is into, may not be what suits you.

I have low blood pressure, which comes with the territory of not being stressed, but when the weather gets hot, my body takes a lot of energy to get the blood around to its enlarged warm veins.

Which brings me to when I tried hot Yoga. Ever heard of it?

It is done in a room that is heated to 39 degrees Celsius with a humidity percentage of about 90 %.

It makes you sweat.

A lot.

People don't wear much clothing.

My neighbouring mat was about 10cm from mine.

The fellow next to me moved his head and shared his sweat with me.

For some reason, that I'm sure to find out one day, people absolutely love it.

I walked out, one, because I couldn't stand the smell of the old sweat in the carpeted floor and two, because I was so dizzy that I has was finding it hard to stand up, I even tried to get out through the storage door, I was that disorientated.

Find something that suits you my friend.

Hot Yoga clearly doesn't float my boat, but it does for thousands of others.

Sometimes it's good to zone out when you're exercising, especially on a walking/running machine or bike. Just like my friend above when she swims, it can be a way to just let the thoughts drift around, without having to be anywhere or really do anything about them, especially when you have your favourite tunes to listen to.

This is also a time to practise mindfulness, allow the thoughts to come and go, but don't follow them too much, we have all seen those unfortunate videos that go viral of people losing their focus on the walking machines and flying off the end.

Another one of my friends uses her exercise time to 'walk my shit out' she says. She uses this time to go over the thoughts that are bothering her and to try and work some of the stuff out.

Whatever you are doing, bring all of your mind to it. Create this space for yourself to be fully present in the moment.

The other day I went on a mindful meditation walk.

I felt the Earth underneath my feet, was it soft, hard, spongy? I felt the wind on my cheeks, I stopped and looked at the leaves and the trees around me. I walked as silently as possible so I could listen to the movement of the earth underneath me, the birds in the trees, the sound of the kangaroos jumping through the bush, the leaves moving in the trees.

Mindfulness in exercise is just bringing ALL of your senses together and being fully present. When I found that my mind wondered off, I gently reminded myself to be in the moment.

I wonder if you could try this next time you go for a walk? Feel the muscles that you use, feel the movement of your feet, feel the motion of your body.

How can being mindful in your exercise increase your fitness, help you lose weight and allow you to enjoy it more?

When you are mindfully exercising, you are more aware of the muscles that you are using, you are creating a stronger body/mind connection and you will feel as though you have a deeper connection to the accomplishments that you are making. When you are aware of the specific movements of your body, you will improve the quality of the movement and a better understanding of how this affects your life. You will feel more in touch with your muscles and body and will really try to do things that make it feel good. This will bring about a snowball effect, increasing the feel good hormones, therefore increasing the enjoyability of the exercise, then you will want to exercise more, and you will continue increasing your fitness levels.

It's a win win situation!

Another benefit of mindfulness in exercise is you will be conscious to move your body in a safe way, you may feel as though on a particular day you need to ramp up the motion on your body and really get your heart beat up and sweat, on other days, you may find your beautiful body needs a really good stretch, or perhaps a combination of both.

Which ever way you decide, always rest afterwards. Take some time for your body to take in the goodness of the exercise you have given it. After exercise you will have a gorgeous rush of endorphins throughout your system, and this will give you a feel good feeling. Enjoy it! Spend some time feeling it entirely with all of your senses and your body will LOVE you for it. Your body will remember that delicious feeling and want more, and next time you exercise, it will be easier to get into the flow.

A combination of different types of workouts is the best way to promote overall wellness in your body. Our bodies get used to one exercise, and you will either have to bump up your routine, or swap to something else to get the continued benefits. After 6 years of teaching 8 classes of Yoga a week and my own practise, my body felt stronger and more flexible than it had ever been…

then I went to a reformer Pilates class, and worked muscles that I hadn't used in my Yoga practise.

Sheesh was I sore for the next couple of days! I really enjoyed it though and it showed me the areas that I needed to focus on for a while.

Please don't make your fitness a stress in your life. No need to berate yourself if you haven't done any fitness for ages, just remember to be in the present moment, the past doesn't exist anymore.

THIS is the only moment to think about.

Plan your day to walk a little, ride a little, move a little. The next day, make that little bit, a little bit more.

Sometimes it's good to have a purpose to your fitness routine, it gives the mind something to focus on and creates a challenge for your body. Maybe walking to a particular light pole for 1 week, and then increase this by 3 more light poles the next week.

Perhaps time yourself and try to get quicker.

Maybe challenge yourself with a different pose or a different type of yoga.

It's good to remember why you are exercising. Some people exercise only when they think they need to lose weight. This could possibly be a great byproduct, but wouldn't it be great if you were exercising because it makes you feel better?

Or because it increases your metabolism and you are regular?

Or it helps you sleep better at night?

It makes you feel really good about yourself and you have a glow to your skin from healthy living? You have more energy throughout your day and you can play chasey with the kids?

Your stress levels and blood pressure go down when you are healthy and fit?

I mentioned at the beginning of this chapter our fitness routine will change throughout our lives. We certainly don't need 'tummy time' to strengthen our backs like we needed before we could crawl...or maybe some of us do! There is no point in saying to yourself, oh, I used to be able to go to the gym after work, but now I have to pick up the kids and cook dinner for them and I don't have time to exercise.

This kind of thinking makes you feel really disgruntled with your life. But, when we think about it as the 'tummy time' example, and we can change things to suit ourselves, let's make exercise into something that fits our lives now.

You may still need this time to yourself and go to the gym for your own mental sanity, but there are other ways to build fitness into your everyday life.

Go for a bike ride with the kids, play frisbee, make a training circuit at home, dance in the kitchen, do Yoga at home, practise your handstands in the park, go for a walk while you're waiting to pick the kids up from afternoon sports, join a pram walking group, jump on the trampoline, join in a neighbourhood cricket/soccer game, do an early morning bootcamp before school and work, play tennis/squash/football/netball/ping pong, do a couple of laps in the pool while your children are are their lessons, find a lunchtime class and remember to pack your clothes the night before so there's no excuses.

There's a saying 'monkey sees, monkey does', now by no means am I calling our beautiful babies monkeys, I just used that sentence so it will hopefully stick in your head.

Your kids are clever.

They see a lot.

You are their first teachers and the most important people in their lives and always will be. As you show them the important things in your life, it will become important to them also, when they are young and as they continue into adulthood.

What a fabulous lesson you have taught them to maintain their health, just by maintaining yours.

In the past we haven't known how additive and medically toxic refined sugar is. The rate of Type 2 Diabetes has risen incredibly over the past couple of years and is becoming a huge worldwide issue. The patterns that we set up now for our kids are important, I believe that some people are only just starting to realise this. If we show our kids that being physically active is important and fun for us, it will be for them also.

Of course, there are always going to be those times the kids aren't going to do anything you say, especially when they are going through those toddler and teenage hormonal stages when they are seeing how far they can push the boundaries, but usually, we can guarantee they are watching and listening to everything you do and say and are taking it in.

Let's give them a healthy start in life by showing them the way.

Be involved with their sporting groups, support them, give them a chance to run and play everyday, limit screen time and give them ideas on how to move in a fun way.

Some kids seem to be incredibly happy to spend all of their time outside playing, mine aren't. I have to monitor their screen time closely and really encourage (bribe) them to go outside and play. But once we are outside climbing across the rocks, playing cricket, riding bikes, practising hockey, chopping wood, swimming, they have an absolute ball.

As mentioned in the previous chapter, Yogis have an ethical philosophy that we can choose to follow. Along with the Yamas, are the Niyamas, which are a way of cultivating self-confidence in a very practical sense.

When practising Yoga, I feel as though I am giving my body a massage from within, it detoxifies my body and spring cleans the insides. This relates to the Niyama cleanliness (Shaucha), on the inside and the outsides of our bodies.

As I like my personal Yoga practise to include quite a sweat inducing workout, a stretch and a meditation, I am practising contentment (Santosha), heat and discipline (Tapas), reflection (Svadhyaya) and the blissful feeling at the end of my practise of self-surrender (Ishvara Pranidhana).

CHAPTER 5

❖

The voices in your head

If people are speaking about you behind your back, then just fart.

I wish the voices in my head wouldn't all speak at the same time. Anon

The conversations that we have in our heads can be horrendous.

We can speak to ourselves in such a derogatory way, and we wouldn't ever *think* of speaking to other people that way, so why do we think it's OK to talk to ourselves in a negative way?

Our negative thought patterns can be changed, but we need to recognise that they are just thoughts before we change them.

Let's imagine our thoughts are words we are reading in our minds. What are words made up of? Letters? What are letters? Wiggles that we have been taught are meaningful when we are younger and learning to read. These wiggles are different in every language, but they really are only marks on a page.

Imagine that the thoughts in your mind are words. They are only marks on your mind. They aren't physical and they can be changed, just like letters can be changed or rubbed out. As an Early Childhood specialist, I know that nearly ALL of our thoughts about who we are, what we stand for, who our families are and what they believe, our ethics, or self belief, just about everything, is imprinted into your mind, wait for it, before you turn 4. Nope, not 14, 40, 44, 104, but 4 years old. Makes you think about what you have said to your kids doesn't it? Makes you think about what has been said to you.

We are born with the spectacular ability to learn any language, it's the repetition that instills the mother tongue into us. It's the same with our thoughts, it's the repetition that forms those thoughts. If we hear over and over the click consonants of the Khoikhoi and the San (Bushmen) tribes in southern Africa, we will develop the ability to speak this language.

If you do not grow up listening to this, you will not have the innate ability to produce this phoneme, although you may be able to mimic it.

It's the same with thoughts, if we hear over and over that we have pudgy thighs (babies with pudgy thighs are totally gorgeous in my opinion), we may take this into our adult lives, and believe we will always have pudgy thighs. Can you see this is a little silly? Most of us lose that baby fat and we develop muscles in our legs as we start to walk. Do we need to keep this belief our thighs are all squishy and lacking in muscle tone? Do we actually start to believe this and create this situation for our bodies to manifest this belief?

Our thoughts are remarkably powerful tools. In my workshops I talk about an incredibly famous and powerful experiment that Japanese scientist **Masaru Emoto** completed. He claimed that thoughts have an effect on the molecular structure of water. He collected water samples and either repeated positive/negative words or pasted messages onto the jars. The most amazing things happened. The crystals in the water that had the negative words spoken repeatedly to it, turned into nasty looking crystals with no apparent form and structure. The crystals in the water that had positive words spoken to it, made the most beautifully formed crystals.

'According to Dr. Jeffrey Utz, Neuroscience, paediatrics, Allegheny University, different people have different percentages of their bodies made up of water. Babies have the most, being born at with about **78%**. By one year of age, that amount drops to about **65%**. In adult men, about **60%** of their bodies are water.'

water.usgs.gov

So babies are 78% water and we now know most of our self learning comes before we are 4.

We also know that negative talk can affect the molecular structure of water, therefore affecting the molecular structure of our bodies.

Pretty full on stuff!

But before we all get our freak on, let's just take a nice slow deep breath.

Firstly, due to the magical evolution (can those words go together?) of neuroscience, we know that we can change our thought patterns.

We don't have to keep the thoughts we grew up with.

So what do you want your thoughts to be?

You have the driver's seat here, you're an adult. For sure, for sure, you can keep believing that you have pudgy thighs, or every time you go into a hardware store you have to do a poo (that was my kids, how about yours?), but it's your choice.

You can also choose to believe you have the most beautiful eyelashes and your neck smells like breast milk, whatever, it's up to you, my friend.

In Miracles Now: 108 Life-Changing Tools for Less Stress, More Flow, and Finding Your True Purpose by Gabrielle Bernstein, she mentions quite a snappy exercise to, firstly, recognise negative thoughts, and secondly, to quite literally 'snap' yourself out of it.

She says to put a rubber band around your wrist and every time you have a negative thought, you snap the band against your wrist. It can seem quite harsh, but what are those negative thoughts doing to your mind that you can't physically see? Or you may be actually able to physically see them.

Do you worry about what people are going to think of you, and start saying things like: 'I'm not good enough for this, I'm always wearing the wrong thing and I should lose 10 kgs, I need to cover up these pudgy thighs'… Then your heart starts racing, your hands get sweaty, your breathing gets shallow, producing very physical side effects from your thoughts.

Whatever you are worried about hasn't even happened yet, why are you sweating about it?

You could use the 'snap' exercise from Gabby and maybe acknowledge that these thoughts are negative and they aren't serving you at this time of your life, you could even think about changing them to 'I am good enough, I can wear whatever I like because when I wear comfortable things that suit me, I feel powerful, confident and attractive.' Even saying this to yourself, you seem to stand up taller, bring your chest out and take deeper breaths. All of this is going to set you up for success, and your kids will watch this transformation and mimic you.

How to get a bikini body.
Get a bikini. Put it on your body.

There are other ways to combat negative self talk, one of them being to acknowledge, call it for what it is, and move on.

For example, as an entrepreneur I am always coming up with ways to create and get my message across to the world. Sometimes it's good, sometimes it's a total failure.

A friend said once 'do you know what I admire about you, it is you have had so many down times in your life, but you just continue to pick yourself up.'

Recently I spent many, many hours putting together what marketers call 'a launch'. It is an enormous amount of work.

I was launching a new e-course.

Not one single person signed up.

So I had a few choices; going a complete downhill roll and say 'fuck it', I give up, clearly everybody hates me and they think I have nothing to teach them, which actually happened for a few days, although this could have been exhaustion from the weeks of preparation I had put into it. After a few wines, meditations, laughs and cuddles from my kids, kitchen dancing and long walks along the beach, I started to get my mojo back, and recognised that not everybody hates me.

I have helped a lot of people, I know what I'm talking about, so let's see why this didn't work.

So I acknowledged it was negative self talk, I called it for what it really was, (my tribe didn't want an online course) and I moved on, (decided to make it into a real book, and you're reading it. Thank you xx)

Having positive self talk isn't about being up yourself.

It is about knowing your strengths and using them for the greater good. I know my weaknesses and I will ask for help, I know my strengths and I will use them to help you.

Can we not judge ourselves when we say this? I'm not judging myself when I say that I have a weakness in maths, there is no judgement. I travelled a lot as a child, and I know I missed out on a lot of learning, that I'm mathematically dyslexic, give me a list of numbers and I'll read them to you in the wrong order. No matter, I don't need to be awesome at everything, neither do you, we just need to know our areas of strengths and focus on these.

Can you ask yourself, with no judgement, what are my strengths and what are my weaknesses?

Another technique that may help you recognise the negative talk is to give that voice a name, no….preferably not your Mother In Law's name, but perhaps a silly, made up name,

'The Grinch' or 'nagging noo noo'.

"Here comes Nagging noo noo again, putting a damper on everything, quick let's get out of the way and maybe she won't see us!" and you skip off to another place in your mind.

Once we have recognised these negative self patterns in ourselves, we can start watching what we say to our beautiful children.

I sometimes feel that I am quite harsh to my kids, I expect respect and I respect them.

As you know my son was born very ill and it would have been easy to give excuses for his behaviour and put it down to his sickness.

Once he got older and I knew that he was able to start controlling his behaviour and had the ability to use emotional language, he still had to behave or face the consequences, as his older sister had to. They knew the rules and when they decided to push those boundaries, I followed the 1,2,3 method and they were put into time-out if, and when, they got to 3.

It's called 1,2,3 Magic parenting method if you are interested in looking into it I will put a link in the resource section. It still is working currently and my kids are 8 and 10.

I hear a lot of different types of parenting methods and I will never judge anyone over what they do, we don't know what the parents have been though.

I know there was a time after 6 months of a sick vomiting screaming child and a small toddler, I was willing to totally loose it. This was when I asked for help, a lot of help.

Friends came over, my son was taken away for a night and my family flew from all over the world to spend some time with us. For this, my son, my daughter, my hubby and I will be eternally grateful. It didn't stop the vomiting and screaming, but physically I got more than 20 minutes sleep in a row and I had the psychological feeling of support, which is incredibly powerful.

When you angrily speak to your kids, just pause for a second and think about it.

Are you really going to break their leg if they 'step one more step'?

Are you really going to go home 'right now if you don't start behaving?' You have to be willing to follow through with your disciplinary technique, or your child will know they don't have to do what you say because you can't follow through.

My kids have had to sit on the side of the road next to my car because they didn't stop screaming at each other. It really freaked out a poor walker at the time.

I *did* leave the shopping trolley half full and drive home to put one of my kids into time out when they had a paddy in the supermarket. And we *did* go back and continued our shopping.

I know I'm heading into the teenage years and my daughter is already showing signs of hormonal surges (is that a nice way of saying complete melt down?), so I am asking my friends who have been though it, the friends I look up to and respect and I'll do my best. One of the best pieces of advice I received is to set a good foundation. I worked really hard at building a strong base for respectful relationships in our household and I am already reaping the benefits. In saying this, it's never too late to start. In the past

2 days I have had the same comment; 'is it always so calm in your house or are you just putting it on because we are here?' Answer; 'no, it's not always this calm, but this the norm, not a show.'

What happens if your kids are the ones with the negative self talk? This can be a time where we can judge ourselves, but is this really helpful for them?

This isn't about you, it's about them. My son told me a couple of years ago that he didn't want to live. What a shock. I had to really sit down with him and listen what was going on, without putting my own spin on it. It turned out to be something completely different to what I assumed he was saying, but very important to him none the less.

We need to actively listen.
With our ears, and eyes.

Our eyes can't be looking at a screen when our children are talking to us. Be at their eye level, look at them and listen.

Children have active minds, if we listen to them they have awesome stories. These stories can give us an amazing understanding about what is happening in their heads, but it may take some time and we may have to either ask the right questions, or not ask anything at all and just listen.

Our children are complex and all different. Some can be more anxious than others.

I have together a guided mediation that may help your child.

They can be downloaded here: http://www.victoriasplaceonline.com.au/?p=1970

This will help your child calm their anxious thoughts by focussing on their breath.

Using the breath is an easy tool for them to remember and can be used in any situation.

Another great tool to use with children is EFT, Emotional Freedom Technique. After a few years of scepticism with this technique, I have come back to it with a wider knowledge base, and I have personally had great successes using it. I will give you a few good resources in the Resource section.

EFT for children is a simple procedure involving tapping on certain points of the body to alleviate 'stuck' emotions.

I was taught this plan as an adult, but I believe it would be a great technique to teach children.

It's the STOP technique.

S: Stop and breath.
T: Listen to your thoughts and see which ones are actually true/useful.
O: Think of other (helpful) thoughts.
P: Plan what to do

Before you teach your beautiful child this technique, you may need to establish that they know what a thought is, as opposed to a feeling.

The most obvious way to do this is to speak to your child about thoughts and feelings, it is a wonderful way of developing their emotional language.

When you are reading a story to them, perhaps point to a characters head and ask 'what do you think he's feeling?'. Feelings are sometimes easier to express. When you think your child is showing this empathy and they can explain feelings, then move onto thoughts; 'what do you think he's thinking?'

CHAPTER 6

I love myself

Dear stress,
I think it's time we broke up.
Love me.

I watched my daughter run through the hallway, suddenly stop and come back to the mirror, doing a great impression of the Fonzy fingers (showing my age...), claim 'You're Awesome!', and proceed to run back down the hallway.

When did we stop giving ourselves compliments in the mirror and start judging every single thing that we think is 'wrong'?

When did we stop telling ourselves 'we're awesome,' and started judging and speaking negatively to ourselves?

I wonder if it's when we started believing others' opinions of us? Remember my experience with the nurse with the headache. It wasn't about me, it was her problem. Or do we believe the opinions of marketing and advertising?

In order to be appealing and sexy, you HAVE to look like this, wear this, make this much money, have this job, be a super-parent, be an amazing lover etc etc...

It all comes back to how much we respect ourselves.

I believe that one of the hardest and most powerful techniques for self-love is the 'mirror technique' that Louise Hay teaches. Ref: www.healyourlife.com/ **mirror-mirror**-on-the-wall.

When I first heard how powerful this technique was, I had just started my self-love journey, I didn't really know that's what it was at the time.

I realised that I hadn't looked properly in a mirror for years and years.

I didn't have any mirrors in my bedroom and I put on the little amount of makeup I used with the steam from the shower on the bathroom mirror so I couldn't see my face. When I went to the hair dressers, I was careful never to look at myself.

This was all a subconscious thinking, not deliberate.

So can you imagine this...

I was lying in bed with a hum dinger of a hangover, feeling like shit and knowing that I needed to do something, so I downloaded Louise Hay's App on my phone and dutifully (I had read that you didn't have to even believe what you say when you start, the magic still happens over time) repeated positive affirmations about myself. It's a pretty App, so I was holding my phone close to my face reading the affirmations when suddenly I was faced with my own reflection!

Arrrhhhh! Panda eyes from my unclean face from the night before, bloodshot and squinting peep holes staring at me. The App turns into a mirror!

I just about threw my phone across the room, it certainly jump started my heart! What a horror to see myself in that state.

So I dare you to try the mirror technique, no, I double dare ya!

Technique 1.

Stand at the biggest mirror you have and look into your eyes (even this part was hard for me) and say out loud: I am willing to change.

Notice, without judgement or emotion, how you feel, does your body react in any way? Now say 'I love you unconditionally' ten times.

This is what my editor wrote in here: "HaHa, I just did that, saying 'I love you unconditionally, and your body is awesome for a 70 year old'. But I couldn't stop giggling, and completely cracked up. Still managed to get to 10 times though! Certainly cheered me up!"

Again notice any reactions you have. No matter what, they are normal and you are normal. I challenge you do this every single day for a month and see what magic happens. Last night, a friend texted me saying she was sick of trying and not losing weight. I texted this technique back and she said; 'I love myself, I'm just lazy.'

When we love ourselves, we will treat our bodies like the temple that they are.

We will love ourselves enough to feed it with fresh and delicious foods, we will move our bodies more, because we know it makes our bodies feel great, and because we love ourselves, we will want to treat it well, it's a win-win situation.

If you or your children have a special person that they look up to, a role model, who has done particularly well for themselves, in any field, you will find that they use, or have used this technique. They positively self-talk to themselves in front of a mirror. Sometimes it seems the most public of these positive self-talkers are the boxers! (Can you hear them in your head? 'I am the greatest!')

After a couple of weeks, you may not feel any different, but you may notice some of your choices are different.

After a month, you may feel more confident and people may start noticing that something is changing within you. When you find this a routine, regular part of your day, this is where the magic is. You will respect yourself more and people will start to notice.

I can't tell you how many people have said 'Gosh Vic, you're glowing!' I also found that a lot of the more negative people in my life made it very clear I had changed and they didn't want anything to do with me. At first, this was very hard to deal with, but then I realised that it was their journey to be on and nothing to do with me, and it's best that I'm not part of their lives at the moment, maybe in the future this will change.

If you don't love yourself first and fall into an unhealthy heap, who is going to look after your family/job/animals etc?

You are the glue that holds everything together. Just like the airline people say; "If there is an emergency, please put your own mask on before you take care of anyone else."

So I can give you a huge list of self help techniques, but will you enjoy them and come back feeling refreshed and able to cope with everything?

Or will you spend the time feeling guilty and not enjoying yourself at all?

I think we all know how we want to feel and we all know that it's better for us and our families if we enjoy ourselves and rejuvenate.

It's a mindset. If you have feelings of guilt for taking some time out for yourself, start small and work up to longer times. This will give your families time to adjust.

Technique 2.

You may not want to start with a week away, maybe just a 10 minute bath. I have recorded some beautiful meditations and they are great to listen to in the bath with an eye pillow on, some nice scents and a locked door. Let everyone know that you will be back to deal with their needs soon. It's nice for our families to see that we appreciate ourselves and they will follow suit.

Technique 3.

Guided meditations are an awesome way to steady the brain. If you are like the hundreds of people that have said to me 'I can't stop my thoughts', try this quick technique.

Take a thought that has been bugging you little, not a huge one, just a little niggle. Take four long seconds to breathe in, hold that breath in for four long seconds, as you slowly breath out, feel the air move slowly from your belly, in your chest, behind your nose, through your nose, now take two slow breaths in and out through your nose.

Did you think about your previous thought? Probably not. That was at least 20 seconds of you controlling your thoughts, all you need now is more practise.

There are many scientific studies to show how beneficial regular meditation is for your mental well-being and they have also found now that the grey matter in your brain is actually strengthened as you grow older if you meditate.

In November 2005, a study published in the journal NeuroReport followed twenty participants from average walks of life in meditation research. Ref: Lazar SW, et al (2005 November 28) Meditation experience is associated with increased cortical thickness. Neuroreport 16(17):1893-1897.

People were given mindful meditation practises each day for forty minutes. The study showed that one hundred percent of the people showed an increase in the grey matter of their brain.

If you are like many of us and the thought of quieting your mind seems impossible, then I would suggest a guided meditation, its really just like listening to a bed-time story being read to you, very lovely indeed.

At a recent relaxation workshop I asked what the participants gained from participating. Most mentioned the 'square breathing' during the meditation was very beneficial for them.

The last participant to comment quietly said;

"I'm sorry, I don't remember any square breathing, all I could think was 'why is Victoria speaking in my dream?'"

I had given her a lovely rest, just like the title of this book.

Here is a link to a square breathing exercise: http://www.victoriasplaceonline.com.au/?p=1836

This has been very beneficial for people who are going through trauma and something that we teach in Yoga therapy for breast cancer.

Technique 4.

Another incredibly powerful technique is gratitude.

My second bub was born 10 pounds, I have stretch marks and wobbly bits. I could look in the mirror and hate my body, especially with all the scarring on my stomach from my operations.

I look at the stomach scars and I am thankful for being alive and I look at my stretch marks and wobbly bits with incredible gratitude for being blessed to be able to have children.

Using gratitude for self love doesn't have to involve physically doing anything. You don't need more time or money to start practising now.

Just stop and look around you.

Can you be grateful for what you are sitting on and love it?

Being able to have the education to read these words and love yourself enough to make positive changes in your life?

For the clothes that you are wearing.

The roof over your head.

The bills that come, because someone knows that you are able to pay them. Just 1 minute of gratitude is a great way to start practising self love. (and it makes the bills easier to handle!)

During our teenage years and sometimes earlier now, we all go through self doubt. Some of us are really good at covering this up and some of us wear our hearts on our sleeves and take this doubt (self hatred) into our hearts and bring it into our adult lives.

I wonder if these sensitive people can now see in hindsight what could have been done so they loved themselves and became confident in doing so?

I wonder why many people blame someone in their past for their unhappiness?

If so, is this what you would like to continue to do, or would you like to let go of that emotional chain and become free to really know how awesome you are?

If you want to remember how awesome you are on a very physical level, read an anatomy book. Our bodies are ridiculously complicated and amazing. During the anatomy part of my Yoga training I was constantly in awe.

What goes on inside our bodies involuntarily is frigging outstanding, and that's just the body.

The brain, well, it blows my mind!

When we recognise our bodies as the miracle it is, we may be more inclined to treat ourselves with increased amounts of self love.

Since I have been hanging around people who have finished having their babies, they tell me that they crave same-sex relationships…sheesh, that could be read in a couple of ways!

Let me explain.

You probably know that our bodies go through a series of transitions during our lifetime that keep our humankind alive. For example when we hear our babies cry in the early weeks after birth, our bodies release the hormone oxytocin. Oxytocin causes the cells in the milk-making lobes of your breasts to contract and eject the milk toward the nipple, and your baby can be fed. (If your baby isn't feeding at that moment, the milk may <u>leak or even spray</u>.).

Ref: http://www.babycenter.com

Our hormones change to suit what our bodies need at different times of our lives.(Another amazing part of our creation!) Obviously there are exceptions to this due to complications or illness.

I can almost pinpoint the moment that my body decided that 'time was ticking' and I started seeking a partner for a committed relationship. It's like natures way of keeping the human species alive and reproducing.

Clever Mother Earth, here's a quick outline of the process.

Helen Fisher of Rutgers University in the States has proposed 3 stages of love – lust, attraction and attachment. Each stage might be driven by different hormones and chemicals.

- Lust, driven by the sex hormones testosterone and oestrogen.
- Attraction, driven by adrenaline causing excitement, dopamine causing pleasure and serotonin causing happiness.
- Attachment, driven by oxytocin causing feelings of attachment as mentioned above and vasopressin which is released after sex and is said to form a part of helping us commit to long term relationships.

When our bodies tell us we have enough children, we then find ourselves craving company that understands what is happening to our bodies, so blokes often find a team or club to join and females crave time with each other. This doesn't mean you love your partner less, it's just another transitional phase in life. If you're in this time, your self love may be surrounding yourself with people that really 'get' you and spending quality time with them.

So what have we got so far for ideas for your self love?

Saying we love ourselves regularly, having gratitude, having a bath (or some form of time out that suits you), doing a guided meditation, spending time with those who fill your soul cup and 'get' you.

What about your children? I wonder if the list could look the same.

Telling them that we love them regularly, encouraging them to be grateful and content for the things that they already have within them that are awesome, encouraging them to take some time out doing something they enjoy, having some quiet reflection time, playing with their mates.

Technique 5.

Find something that fills your soul cup. Here are some suggestions.

- Each time someone gives you a compliment, say 'thank you' and either keep it on a physical list or a mental one that you can read anytime you need a reminder.

- Spend time with your friends uplifting and supporting each other.

- I have put together a free home retreat kit with a daily planner, meditations, recipes and lots more. Download it at www.victoriasplaceonline.com.au and enjoy a perfect day/weekend for yourself.

- Practise listening to what fills you with joy and following this path. Listen to what dulled your joy and practise saying 'no.'

- Fill your body with fresh, great food and fresh, clean water.

- Do one of the stretches I have given you in Chapter 10.

- If you are finding everything overwhelming, ask for help. People love to help others, it makes them feel great.

- Run yourself a bath and listen to the self love guided meditation I have put together for you. Download it here: http://www.victoriasplaceonline.com. au/?p=1973

- Put an alarm on that starts your day with a little bit of sparkle.

- Know that YOU are enough and YOU deserve to be loved.

- Spend time in nature with the sun shining on you. Many of us are not getting the Vitamin D that we need these days.

- Write a letter to yourself as a child, saying all of the things that you would have liked to have heard and really love yourself.

- Put on some uplifting music and have your own dance party.

CHAPTER 7

DECLUTTERING

I wish I could Google
for things in my house.

I'm currently making some changes
in my life. If you don't hear from
me, you're one of them. Anon.

I have a members only group called Victoria's VIP's. I
send them a whole shed load of inspiration, including Yoga
and meditation videos, recipes, drinks, relaxation tips and I
call them once a month to help them along their relaxation
journey. Each month I give them a lifestyle challenge.

One particular month was to declutter one part of their
lives. I suggested starting at the underwear drawer. How
many grey old ill-fitting bras and the wrong sized knickers/
jocks do we actually need?

It goes to show that this is a hot topic at the moment, as two of the highest selling books on Amazon are about tidying up.

My house isn't tidy, I'm not a huge fan of excessive housework, but things are clean and when we need to tidy, it's easy, because we have put into place areas for everything. It takes the three of us ten minutes to tidy our small house. One of the reasons my house isn't tidy, is that the kids seem to have a lot of projects on the go, and they like to come back to them periodically, which means that I have to let things flow a little sometimes.

Currently my son is dead keen on drawing and cutting out his favourite characters from a game he plays, and they are everywhere, they even sleep and eat next to him.

My daughter reads a different book in different rooms, no problem, just let it flow.

I am also a huge fan of having a box for charity at all times. Then when we have grown out of something, it goes straight in the box after a wash and it doesn't clutter up our rooms. The box gets emptied regularly.

We also use the library a lot and any books that I buy, I pass onto whoever would like them.

I know that my mind does go a little bananas when I can't walk across the floor and I can't see any table tops. Then we need to have a little chat about respecting each others spaces.

This is why we need to declutter. The space around us can represent what is going on in our minds. As we have spoken about in previous chapters, we don't need to keep the crap that we have been collecting from our past and storing it if it isn't useful for our lives RIGHT NOW.

When we have clear spaces around us, it can give us space for the things that really matter.

Would you prefer to spend your day dusting all of those trinkets or reading your favourite book?

Would you prefer to spend the night ironing the clothes that just hang in your closet and you don't wear, or watching a hilarious movie with your friends and family?

Would you prefer to be picking up hundreds of toys on the floor, or spending quality time with one or two toys? Toy libraries are the bomb. Depending on what policy your local toy library has, you usually get to rent out a couple of toys each month and then give them back. Cool hey? It was great to give me ideas for Christmas presents.

I loved letting my children choose what they wanted without any comment from me, it really amazed me what they chose.

There are many ways to declutter and then to keep things tidy. One of the best advice I got when things seem to be too overwhelming, is to start at the door, turn left and start at the top, don't look at anything else, just start there, it's amazing how much you get through.

As I have mentioned previously, it's incredibly difficult to keep doing something, unless you enjoy it.

Now I don't expect you to be in love with cleaning, but we can make it easier, my family like to turn up the volume on the tunes.

Another way to make things a little easier, is to be mindful when we are cleaning. Bring all of your attention to it. When I am mopping, I think about who and what I can be grateful for; who made the mop? I am grateful I have a house and floors to clean. Who made the floor cleaner and who put it on the shelves of the supermarket? I am grateful that I have hot, hot water to clean with.

I'll give you 10 tips on decluttering and then 10 tips on how to keep things tidy.

1. *Do something each day for 5 minutes.* Perhaps sort the medicine cabinet, your underwear drawer, sort out one bookshelf, organise your shoes, fill a large garbage bag with stuff for charity, recycle all of the newspapers, throw out all of the pens that don't work, clean all or part of your desk at work, go through one shelf of your pantry and throw out anything that is out of date or use what you can quickly, look at your recipe books and see which ones you haven't used for years or see which ones you can find online, go through one shelf in your linen cupboard and donate what you don't use.

2. *Make a game of decluttering for one month.* The first day of the month, throw or give one thing away. The second day of the month, throw or give two things away. On the third day of the month, throw or give three things away, do you see the pattern here? By the time you have completed your 30 day month, you would have thrown or given away 573 things.

3. *Turned every hanger in your wardrobe around the wrong way.* I actually enjoyed doing this one a couple of years ago. I heard about it through social media and decided to try it. Each time I wore something, I put the hanger back facing the correct way. At the end of a year (the blog I read said 3 months, but I decided to lengthen it) I could see what I wear a lot and what I could give to charity or sell. Very easy, very practical, very enlightening.

4. *Have designated spots for everything, then the whole family know where things need to go when they are actually tidying up.* All lego goes here, all books go here, all drawing paper goes here, all textas/pens/ crayons go here, all papers go here, all cleaning products go here.

5. *Put it away.* Have a look at your tables and bench tops. Do you burn that candle very night? Could it be put away until you do? Do you use that griller everyday? Could it be put into a kitchen cupboard? If that vase doesn't have flowers in it, does it really need to be out? Start by clearing one table or bench top and stop and see how it feels. It's quite freeing. The unfortunate thing that happens to me is that as soon as I clear a space, my family thinks it's awesome, and they can dump heaps of stuff there. You may find this too? Perhaps we could have a chat about having a clutter free zone and how it makes you feel when it's messy and how it makes you feel when it's clear.

6. *You may like to have a HUGE declutter party with your family.* Have big boxes around, some for the bin, some for charity and some to sell. Put great music on and treat yourselves with a yummy lunch/dinner, some delicious drinks to keep things going and perhaps a 'treat' day the next day and all do something fun together. Then the next weekend, advertise and have an awesome Garage Sale and get some cashola for all of your hard work.

7. *There are professional de-clutterers that can come into your house and look you in the eye and ask you why you have 46 pens in your drawer.* You may be at a stage where you need another opinion and these people are fantastic at what they do.

8. *When you are sorting things out to move, have an 'I dunno' box.* This is easiest done when you are moving home, but it can also be done when you are having a re-arrange of things/rooms in your house. It's a piece that you don't know whether to throw it out, or to keep it. Pack it in this box and don't undo it until you REALLY need it. After about a year of keeping that box, you will probably have forgotten what is actually in the box. Do you really need to keep it? Go through it and keep what you really need and sell/give away what you haven't used for a year.

9. *Sort it out.* We all have it, I call it my 'shit' draw. It's where all of the stuff goes that doesn't really have a home. It's usually in the kitchen. If you put draw separators in there, like you have in the cutlery

draw, things can be neatly placed there and is so much easier to find.

10. *Now that you have the most Zen looking home and your mind is feeling all free of clutter. Don't clutter it up again.* Just like my family and my zen tabletops, you don't need to rush out and collect more crap that you don't actually use. There's a few techniques to do this, one is to look at the price of the product and see if you feel it is actually worth spending your hard earned cash on, put it down, walk out of the shop and after an hour, see if you still really want it. For bigger purchases, perhaps a longer time in between the actual thought of buying it and the purchase. Some people mention 5 days, others say wait 30 days. Your bank account will love you, you will have more money to spend on other things, like holidays or music, and your home will be easier and quicker to clean. Winner!!!

The method that Marie Kondo uses in her New York Times bestseller list book The Life- Changing Magic of Tidying Up, has a base theory of 'do you love it'? Does this particular thing bring you joy and happiness. If not, you don't need it. She recommends starting with easy things, like I have suggested above, then move onto the more sentimental things later when you are already practised in de-cluttering.

10 Tips to tidy.

1. *Have some routines.* Make the beds each morning and the kids can do their own. Do all those little things that need to be done on a daily basis and just do them routinely. The bench around food preparation always need to be clear (something my husband has had to drill into me), dishes away, space clear of crumbs and not a drop-off zone for anything else.

2. *Have one spot for all of your incoming paperwork and have a time to organise it all.* This stops all the double-handling that we do, for example, instead of picking up the mail, opening it as you stand in the kitchen, putting it 'somewhere' that may or may not be filed and sorted, then spending time finding it again, carving out time to deal with it if it's a bill or a note that has to be signed and then filing it. How about, when you get the mail/school newsletters, put them in one spot next to your computer or better yet, get them all sent by email. Have an allocated time to deal with it each day and pay/reply, then recycle the paper. You don't need to keep anything that you can find online, this includes bank statements and manuals.

3. *This is true for your email inbox as well.* These days most of us have multiple email addresses and we have subscribed to hundreds of things. This can take up a serious amount of time deleting what we don't want. There are programs that can go through all of the subscriptions you have and sort out what

you don't use anymore. This can also be a great savings of money, as many of these can be paid annual subscriptions. Saving you time AND money, cool!

4. While we're at the computer, check out how many duplicates you have. I know I used to have heaps of double ups of photos. With digital photography, some of us take more photos than we will ever look at. Before you download them onto your computer, go through your camera and delete ALL of the ones that you don't want, then delete them from your camera, avoiding double-handling again.

5. *Keep your products together.* I like Shannon Lush's way of cleaning. She's become very famous since I first heard of her and I'm pretty sure I saw her first ever interview about cleaning. What I love about her is she uses natural, inexpensive products and she's very practical. One main thing I took from her is to keep my cleaning materials in the place I'm cleaning, this was a little tricky when I had small children, but now they are older, I can keep all of the bathroom cleaners in the actual bathroom. No need wasting time collecting it all. This is how she speed cleans her bathroom 1-2 minutes :

    "I put a pair of pantyhose over the head of a broom, a scarf on my head, grab my clutter bucket in which I put anything that hasn't got a washable surface (towels, toothpaste, shampoos, etc) and then put that outside the door. I have my bicarb soda in my parmesan cheese shaker, my white vinegar in a spray bottle, I go in with my broom and I pretend I'm a carousel, shaking the bicarb around in a circle. As soon as I start spraying I start sweeping with the broom. I sweep from the ceiling all the way down to the floor. Once done, I rinse the broom and again sweep from ceiling to floor, but this time with just the damp broom to remove any excess bicarb soda. Once every three months, I'll nip any mould growing in the bud by using my oil of clove mixture - that is 1/4 teaspoon oil of cloves per Litre of water, lightly misted around the room. Don't brush off. To clean any glass in your bathroom - don't use newspaper - use paper towel with methylated or white spirits and you're done!

And my personal tip? Have the 1812 Overture blaring in the background - the sound of cannon fire in the background will really get you inspired." Taken from a quote on ABC Radio, interview by Elk Kovaricek called How to clean your bathroom like Shannon Lush.

6. *Multitask.* Every time you prepare to walk from one room to the next, scan quickly to see if there is anything that has moved from its rightful spot that you can take with you. Do the same when going up or downstairs.

7. *Put the dishwasher and the washing machine on overnight so it's finished when you get up in the morning.* Use the time you're not available to do housework, to do housework in a sneaky way! This might mean getting a robot vacuum cleaner.

8. *A lot of people like a schedule for their cleaning.* If you Google 'cleaning schedule' there is such a great variety, you're sure to find something that appeals to your eye and suits your household.

9. *Make your appliances work for YOU.* I opened my Instagram account one day to find a friend had posted a photo of her kids school hats in the dishwasher, what a great way to wash things! Any heavy duty toys, lego, cars, plastic dolls can go in the dishwasher. I tend to put a lot of things in the washing machine, not just clothing.

10. *Hire a Fairy.* We don't anymore, but we used to have a cleaner come and help us out every fortnight. We came home and would say 'oh wonderful, the cleaning fairies have come.' I loved my cleaner. I used to tell her how much she helped my mental health. It was also a great way to get the whole house tidy, we spent the night before she came picking everything up so that she could clean. Now I have moved, I use the rent inspections as a great excuse to do a good spring clean.

CHAPTER 8

Wrapping it all up in love

There's a 6th love language, it's called letting me sleep in.

Ever thought that your partner is speaking a different language, or do they look at you with a confused/blank look when you're trying to explain something?

Have you wondered why a discipline method works for one child, completely flops with the other and they couldn't care less?

Since I have heard about the Five Love Languages, outlined by Dr. Gary Chapman, it has made communicating mindfully so much easier in my house. It has taken out the guess work and I am able to really think about what I am saying, how I am listening and what implications my language and actions have within our household.

I'll list them for you here and then discuss them afterwards. You may like to stop after the list and think about yourself and your loved ones before you move on.

1.   Words of Affirmation.
2.   Quality Time.
3.   Gifts.
4.   Acts of Service.
5.   Physical Touch

As you know there is always an action and a reaction. This is very true for the Love Languages.

Now you know the 5 Love languages, let's get a little deeper.

1.   *Words of Affirmation.* Affirmation these days seems to bring up something you say to yourself, but in this circumstance, it is words that others say to you and what you hear. If this is your love language, you react positively to words and they are incredibly meaningful to you. A flippant or thoughtless comment can send you into a tail-spin and you may ponder on it for an enormous amount of time. If the person giving these messages is not this particular love language, they probably won't understand why you are so upset over something they said. Adults and children with this love language like to hear 'I love you' a lot and with meaning. You will probably recognise this love language easily.

2.   *Quality Time.* This is quite self-explanatory and we have touched on this topic in Chapter 2 when discussing mindfulness. When our love language is quality time, it is undivided attention, without other distractions and really listening and being there for that person. The opposite to this one is obviously

not having quality time with this person. If we take off half way through, or constantly put off spending time with this person, it will upset this person a lot.

3. *Gifts.* When I first heard about this one and realised that this is my daughter, I felt a little confused. I am trying to teach her to be non-materialistic and be grateful for the abundance that we have, but I didn't want her thinking that I didn't love her when I don't give her things. After researching (and using my poor daughter as a guinea pig), I have come to the belief that gifts don't need to be bought gifts. They can be gestures of love, a flower, an serving of their favourite meal. If I was to forget her, it would be heart breaking for her. A perfect example of my daughter being this 'love language' happened only this morning. She was giving a card for her first boyfriend's birthday (they are only 10…I know, I know, but that's another issue all together) and when she went to put it in her school bag, she kept it behind her back so I didn't see what was in it. It turns out that she had put in her whole savings in cash and was going to give it to him at school.

4. *Acts of service.* This is my hubby. If I don't say thank you for his doing something that normally needs to be done, it's devastating in his mind, it has taken me eons to recognise this, as it's not my love language. A perfect example of this is when I interviewed a community worker on love languages, I couldn't find my paperwork about the five love langauges. It turns out that hubby had written me a message on the back of the paperwork and stuck it to my

computer. This is what it said: 'Vik's jobs. Clean, mow and weed shop, weed and mow house, fix computer.' He needed affirmation that I loved him and that I would do this for my family. How ironic that it was written on the back of my list of love languages.

In the past, this type of note would have had me in a spitting, fire breathing dragon type of tizz.

Once you recognise what our partner's love language is, how much easier can your life be?
It is great to be able to let them know what YOUR love language is.

5. *Physical touch*. Now this one is mine, I love touch and crave it. This love language isn't sexual, but the act of physically touching. If I don't get enough touch from my loved ones, I send myself off for a massage, as it refills my soul cup. When I grow up I want to be a cuddle-granny. One of those lovely people that go into hospitals and stroke the premie babies. During my Early Childhood studies at University I learnt that humans have a higher rate of living if they are touched and those poor parents can't be there 24 hours a day. For people that have this as their love language, physical abuse or negative touch is unforgivable.

    Communicating that this is my love language to my husband has changed many things in your our relationship for the better.

I'd like to point out though that we don't necessarily need to put pressure on our loved ones to get what we need. We have other relatives and friends that may be able to fill your soul cup.

I wonder if we are a mixture of these love languages though? I'm not going to claim to be an expert on this, I certainly have a lot to learn about communication and love. If we are mindful about our communication and start to recognise how our loved ones communicate, we can start to really understand how they react to things and how we react. We can recognise what we are not only saying, but how it really affects the other person.

How many times do we hear our friends say 'he just doesn't get me!' Do YOU get yourself?

Which love language are you and have you discussed this with your loved ones?

You may be in the throes of the teenage years and dealing with an overload of emotions and confusion.

We often hear teenagers say about their parents; 'but they just don't get me!'

It may not be in the teenagers' emotional language repertoire to communicate how they are feeling, but as their parents we have grown with them, and we can distinguish how best to communicate with them at this challenging time of their lives.

Are you a little confused about which love language you are? There is a plethora of quizzes you can take to choose. As always, keep an open mind. I believe that we have an overlying love language but as we go through life and things change, we can give and take appreciation/love in a multitude of ways.

Here are some examples of how we can acknowledge our loved ones by using their love language.

Words of Affirmation.

Adults: Using loving words sincerely. 'I love you', 'That was a wonderful thing to do,' 'You look great today'.

Children: 'Thank you, I really appreciate what you did', 'You're a star,' 'I missed you when you were gone.'

Quality Time.

Adults: Turning off the phones, TV and shutting down the computer and spending uninterrupted time chatting. Going for a drive to a place where you haven't been before and spending some time there. Watching a movie together.

Children: When you have more than 1 child, it's nice for your 'quality time' child to be taken out by themselves, even if it is to do some chores with you. Make eye contact and make sure that each day you are turning off any device and really listening to what they have to tell you, even for a short moment. Dinner time is a perfect time for this. Read together regularly.

Gifts.

Adults: Remember what their favourite chocolate bar is and buy it when you're doing your weekly shop, pick them a bunch of flowers from the garden, remember to bring them a token from the place where you've stayed when you go away.

Children: Keep a stash of inexpensive gifts, pick them a flower, leave a small treat for them when you leave for an extended period, ask them to help you buy thoughtful gifts for others, each time you visit the library try to get them the latest book series.

Acts of Service.

Adults: doing an unexpected act of kindness for them, making them a nice meal, washing up the dishes unexpectedly, changing nappies without being asked.

Children: Practice sports/music/crafts together, help with homework or projects, pick them up on time, do one of their chores for them as a surprise, spend time with them serving others.

Physical Touch.

Adults: this one can seem pretty obvious, and often sex is the first thing we think of when this love language is mentioned, but it's so much more than that. It's hugging, massages, kissing, holding hands, cuddling on the couch when watching TV.

Children: Hold hands, cuddle, family tickle time, touch while reading stories or watching movies, teaching children what 'safe' touching is.

See Chapter 12 for more resources on safe touching.

CHAPTER 9

❖

Mala: a heavenly garland

Q: What did the yogi tell his restless student?
A: Don't just do something - Sit there!

I have been mentioning the Yogic philosophy through-out the book and now I am going to thread it all together for you, so you can use it as a beautiful necklace to take with you and wear as a reminder to relax, we call this a Mala.

If you see me you will notice that I wear either a bracelet or necklace each day. This is my physical reminder to slow down, take a breath and move mindfully through-out my day.

These 8 steps of the Yogic philosophy are just guidelines for you, it's up to you to choose what fits into your life and what allows you to shine.

What has this got to do with you?

The Yogic philosophy can work as a life blueprint and structure.

A place where to you can look for guidance when you may be confused. The yogic philosophy doesn't attune itself to any religion or secular way of thinking. You have the ability to build it into your own life the way YOU want it to.

Most people think of people who practise yoga as bendy, pretzel looking waifs, and most of the magazines would love you to think that this is what you should be doing. During a wellness workshop I was teaching, another one of the speakers came up to me and said 'Thank goodness you're normal and bigger than all of those other Yoga teachers'. Yes, I weigh more than I used to do, but I am physically stronger and healthier than I have ever been.

So let's start here shall we, in the bendy/movement side of Yoga, we call it Asana. We have talked about movement in Chapter 4, we all know that we need to move. It's currently trending at the moment to say that we don't need the exercise to lose weight, it's all about the food that we eat. Please don't let this be an excuse to sit on the couch. I believe exercise is for so much more than weight management.

It's about mental health and how you feel about yourself. It's about getting fresh air and your blood pumping around your body. It's about meeting friends and walking the dog. It's about having fun and trying something new. Moving is so much more than exercising. It's creating strong bones for later on in life and keeping your insides healthy. Moving creates these delicious hormones called endorphins, that are literally 'feel good' hormones, and who doesn't want that, right?

But…you're not going to get these feel good hormones if you hate what you're doing, easy solution; find something you like doing!

Another huge part of the Yogic philosophy is breathing, we call it Pranayama. We have discussed breathing ALOT in this book.

Why?

Well, what happens if you don't breathe?

You die.

It's blunt and simple.

I have given you quite a few breathing techniques to use for different times of your life in Chapter 1 and I'll give you more at the end of this chapter.

If we make the most of our breath, we can make the most of our lives.

If we give our beautiful bodies as much clean fresh oxygen as possible, we will be able to give the blood system all the oxygen goodness to make our muscles and internal organs work well and our minds clear.

Speaking about the mind and breathing, a friend of mine reminds me of a great saying when we see each other; 'breathe in the good shit, breathe out the bullshit'.

You may like to put the book down and practise this now?

This leads me into the next part of the philosophy; Pratyahara. (notice I'm not numbering them, you will see them listed, but they all work within one another, so I'm trying not to make one more important than the other.)

This is when we start really looking at what we are doing in our lives and perhaps detaching ourselves from anything that is not beneficial to our health and growth. Here we could look at the foods we put into our bodies and maybe think twice about how much sugar/preservatives we have throughout the day.

We could use this part of the Yogic philosophy to think about what sort of unhealthy thoughts we are putting into our minds and perhaps use the snap technique I have mentioned previously to reign in the negative thoughts.

Following on from this can be the practise of concentration, or Dharana. We need to be vigilant about keeping ourselves well. I know, we will all slip up but it's good to know you have the tools to get back on track. If we practise mindfulness or meditation, we train our minds to concentrate and focus.

This will help you in so many areas of your life, your work, listening to the kids, study.

Our lives are so jam packed with stimulus coming to us in all directions, it's easy to get overwhelmed. We can teach our minds to deal with the distractions and focus on what is important, usually exactly what is in front of you.

When we are totally focussed on what we are doing, we are in a state of Dhyana, or contemplation. Yours may not be meditation, as discussed in Chapter 2, it may be swimming or cooking or painting. We are in Dhyana when we are in a state of keen awareness, without outside stimulus distracting us. In this state, your mind is quiet and peaceful and in this stillness you have little or no thought, you are completely 'in the moment', usually listening to your calm breath.

As you reach this beautiful state of bliss, you have reached Samadhi. I explained this feeling to my kids as 'when you are just about to fall asleep and you're warm and floating with nowhere to go and feeling as though everything is well with the world.' This is a place of perfect peace and relaxation. Often people get to this stage during meditations, and it's such a pleasure to watch. They can hear me, but they can't feel their bodies and they feel as though they are floating. I believe this is where the notion of levitation during meditation comes from, it feels as though you are weightless, in your body and in your mind. You have nothing weighing you down. This state gives the body and mind a delicious rest and allows you to deal with things from a more relaxed state of mind.

One of my favourite sayings is:

"Do unto others as you would have them do unto you."

Yogis call our behaviour to others our Yamas and our behaviours towards ourselves the Niyamas. They are explained in further detail in Chapter 11. These self management tools help us navigate some of the trickier times and are a really good base to come back to when you need them.

If we can manage our own stress and teach our children the gift of self-regulation, it provides us and them with lifelong tools. Self-regulation is an ability to control and navigate our feelings, impulses, and behaviours.

When we are self-regulated, we can both stop or start doing something, even if we don't want to.

We can delay gratification, can think ahead, can control impulses and consider options.

Here are some techniques for you to try.

The first breath is called the 'hissing or teeth breath' (Sitkari Pranayama) and I recommend starting with this one.

Sitkari refers to the sound made by drawing in air, a kind of reversed hissing, like that made when suddenly touching ice or a hot object. The sound is produced while inhaling through the front teeth-either tightly closed or slightly ajar and should be regulated so as to be smooth and sound pleasant.

Technique 1. Hissing breath

1. *Sit comfortably.*
2. *Bring the front teeth together.*
3. *Inhale through your clenched teeth making a hissing sound, and feel the coolness of the breath.*
4. *Exhale through your nostrils, mouth tightly shut.*
5. *Repeat the process all over again.*
6. *Start with 3 rounds then go up to 5, then 10 rounds.*

Sitkari cools not just the mouth, it has a cooling and a relaxing effect on the whole body and mind. It soothes the nervous system and is excellent on a hot day as it eliminates heat and thirst.

This requires us to slow down and concentrate on our breath. Breath awareness is the first stages of becoming mindful.

Technique 2. Humming Breath

This is one of my favourites, sometimes it's called Bee breath (Bhramari Pranayama). This breath is beautifully relaxing and calming. It also works well when children are feeling frustrated, overwhelmed or irritable.

1. *Sit comfortably*
2. *With relaxed arms, place one hand on your belly and one hand on your chest, allow the elbows to be relaxed.*
3. *Take a deep breath in through your nose and hummmmmm on the way out as the breath goes out the nose. Keep your mouth closed.*
   Your body will feel the vibration sound as it relaxes and calms the body and mind.
4. *Do 5 rounds.*

Humming breath is traditionally done with the hands over the ears; give it a go, it feels really cool. (I was in a Yoga class mentoring a teacher during her training, and she asked the class to do bee breath, we got a few buzzing sounds and had to suppress a little giggle.)

Technique 3. Using your breath to dissolve a thought.

Breath in deeply though your nose 1,2,3,4
Breath out fully through your mouth 1,2,3,4
As your mind starts forming thoughts, imagine that the thought is a cloud above your head.
As you breath in 1,2,3,4, notice this cloud above your head.
As you breath out 1,2,3,4 let the cloud dissolve.
Repeat 3 times.

CHAPTER 10

Asana (poses)

Sink your front thigh deeper and
think to yourself, what if the Hokey
Pokey really *is* what it's all about.
Yoga teacher.

It is my belief that Yoga is one of the best ways to keep
yourself fit and healthy and 6000 years of history can back
that up.

Here is a simple sequence that you may like to try. You
need to really listen to your own body and see if the pose is
right for you. Obviously if you have sore knees, don't lean on
them or put a blanket underneath them. If you find yourself
holding your breath, release it, and ask yourself if you are
pushing the pose too much. Hold the poses for 30 seconds,
or more if you wish to.

Yoga is not about pain, if you feel pain, stop.

1. Start by coming onto your hands and knees. Bring the hands directly under the shoulders and knees directly under your hips. Feel to see if your balance is in the middle. Engage the muscles in your tummy and do a few rounds of belly breathing, feeling the movement of your belly.

2. Gently bring the belly in towards the spine and start to curl the upper spine up towards the sky, at the same time tuck the chin towards the chest and bring the pelvis and forehead towards each other.

3. Then move in the opposite way. Bring the tailbone and crown of the head towards the sky, and belly towards the floor. This is cat/cow pose. This is a wonderful way to release the spine each morning.

4. Come back to a straight spine and then move your bottom towards your heels, resting your belly on your thighs and your forehead on the floor. If your head doesn't touch the floor, bring your hands underneath, so it takes the pressure off the back of your neck. Rest here feeling the belly moving as you breathe. See where your arms are more comfortable, and if you feel a little suffocated in this pose, allow the knees to come wide and the toes come together and rest in between your legs.

5. Come onto your hands and knees again. Bringing the belly in to balance you, stretch your right leg out straight behind you, no higher than the hip. Remember to breathe. If your balance is OK here, stretch out the leg arm straight in front of you. Stay here steadily for as long as you wish, then swap sides.

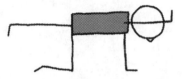

6. Come to standing and feel if you're balanced on both sides of your body and the front and the back, have a little rock from side to side and feel the balance settle into your body. Soften the shoulders and lengthen yourself up towards the sky, while you press your feet into the floor.

7. Take a breath in and as you breath out start to bend forward leading with the crown the head, bending at the hips, not the waist. Gently bring your torso down and rest. Breath in and lengthen your spine and breathe out and fold forward. Stay here for as long as you like.

8. Placing your hands on the ground either side of your feet, bring the right foot back. **Check that you front knee is directly on top or behind your front foot.** Stay here with your hands on the ground, or stretch them up to the sky.

9. Bring your left foot back to meet your right foot and allow your body to be in a straight line, you may like to place the knees on the ground.

10. Bend your elbows and keeping them tucked into the body, bring your torso and knees down to the floor.

11. Push your body forward and press on your hands. Lift your chest forwards and the crown of the head to the ceiling. Do not push your chin out, it puts too much pressure on your neck.

12. Pushing on your hands, lift the bottom high into the air. Push the finger pads and knuckles into the floor, taking the pressure off the wrists. Push the heels towards the ground. Keep the knees a little soft and relax the back of the neck.

13. Walk the feet towards the hands and fold forwards again from the hip crease.

14. Straighten your back and place your hands on your thighs.

15. On your next breath in, come to standing.
    Repeat this sequence from No. 6 stepping back the left foot this time.

16. Come to a cross legged sitting position. Place one hand on the floor next to you and lift the opposite arm towards the sky and stretch it over your head towards the opposite wall. Swap sides.

17. Bring your hands together in front of you and roll your wrists and circles both ways. Lift your arms above your head, trying to keep the chest directly over the pelvis.

18. Place your hands behind you and stretch your chest towards the sky.

19. Place your hands on your knees and do some nice neck rolls.

20. Place your right hand beside you and left hand on right knee. Lift your spine and engage the muscles in your belly. Gently start twisting from the waist, the chest, the shoulders, the neck, the chin, the nose, the eyes, the forehead. Come back in reverse. Swap to the other side.

21. This pose is the most important. Rest on your back with your feet relaxed out to the sides, or arms relaxed with 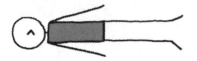 the palms of your hands facing upwards. Do belly breathing and then listen to a guided relaxation.

If you have problems getting up and down from the floor, I have designed a Chair Yoga Card Deck for you. Here are some of the poses that you get, they are great to do by themselves as a quick stretch, or using one of the sequences you get free with the card deck.

1. Wrist Stretch.

Bring both arms in front of you, palms facing out.

Hold the fingers of one hand and stretch them back towards the forearm for 10 sec.

Lower hand and push the back of the hand, fingers towards the underneath of the arm, hold 10 secs.

Swap

2. Forward Bend.

Relax your face, shoulders and arms.

Place your feet firmly on the ground.

Gently roll forwards until your reach your edge.

Breath in and lengthen your spine, breath out and relax further forward. X 5.

3. Back Bend.

Hold the back of the chair.

Bring your chin towards your chest.

Bring the chest toward and the tail bone to the back of the chair.

Hold for 10 secs. X 5

4. Hip Opener.

Place one ankle on top of the knee.

Press the knee down.

Hold for 10 secs.

Swap X 5.

5. Ankle Rotation.

Sit straight in the chair.

Lift one leg and draw circles with the toes, allowing the ankle to rotate 5 times.

Rotate the other way 5 times.

Swap legs.

All the links for my wellness products and your freebies are in the the recommended reading section.

Images Sourced with permission from George Watts www. GeorgeWatts.org.

CHAPTER 11

Singing in the street

'Can you lick your back?'

We are all different, but so, so alike.

During my Yoga teacher training I wanted to walk down the street yelling at the top of my lungs...'OH MY GODDESS!!! I have found THE answer to all of life's questions and problems!' I wanted to shake people and say *'follow the Yogic philosophy, and you can't go wrong! Do the Asana (stretches/strength training), do the meditations, follow the lifestyle observances and you will find a life of complete bliss!'*.

Can you imagine?

At the time of my Yoga teacher training I was living in a small rural country town in Western Australia.

When I enquired about hiring a hall to teach Yoga, the answer was,

'Oh no, you can't have people doing THAT kind of thing here.'

Everyone would have thought I was nuts and may have strapped me to the nearest combine harvester and driven me out of town as fast as the humungous machine could go.

When I told my husband's tradie friends, they said 'oh yeah, Yoga, there's a magazine in a toilet about that. It's what Sting does with his wife isn't it?'

I was also asked a few times if I could lick my back (hmmm, do I want to?) and 'so…(with suggestive fuzzy mono-brow flickering) you know ALL the positions do you, want to show me? (more caterpillar crawling on the forehead movements) and another, not so PC, reference to my book title.

I now go with the flow and wait till the student is ready for the teacher. I have found there is no point trying to help someone who doesn't want your help, all you can do is inspire them through your own lifestyle and then they can choose to make a change.

So if you choose to and it makes it more exciting for you, you can imagine me running up and down a small town country street clapping, jingling and singing the following Yogic self observances; the Yamas and Niyamas.

Nonviolence, <u>Ahimsa</u>
Truthfulness, Satya
Non-stealing, Asteya
Restraint, Brahmacharya
Non covetousness (not being materialistic), Aparigraha

Cleanliness, Saucha
Contentment, Santosa
Spiritual practises, Tapas
Study of history and of one's self, Svadhyaya
Surrender to God/a higher being, Isvara pranidhana.

The philosophy of Yoga has been around since the sixth and fifth centuries BCE, does it sounds a little familiar to you?

Here's where you may have heard some of it before;

The 10 Commandments.

The last 6 have similarities to the Yogic philosophy.
　You shall not murder.
　You shall not commit adultery.
　You shall not steal.
　You shall not bear false witness against your neighbour.
　You shall not covet.

It seems that no matter what our spiritual belief system is, they are all so similar that maybe, perhaps, we could all accept that we all want the same thing out of life?

It all boils down to one big happy pot of peacefulness and content.

Am I stirring the pot? Maybe.

Let's imagine that we are all standing around the said pot, we all have a spoon and we are all contributing to what goes into the broth that feeds YOUR soul and everyone else's on the planet, now and whoever else will be here in the future.

What colour is your pot? Mine's one of those huge old cast iron ones and I have a large old wooden spoon that is stained with the history of previous delicious meals and memories.

I'm outside at night with you, the sky is a velvety blanket with bright shiny stars surrounding us.

The ingredient I choose to place into our broth is contentment.

What's yours?

Here are some ideas; peace, truth, honesty, self control, sharing, respect, continual learning, individuality and regard for differences, self improvement, spiritual acceptance and tolerance.

How do we explain these life observances to our children?

Well the work is already done for you.

Have a look at any sandpit or Kindergarten.

You will inevitably find a sign that reads much like this one;

Be respectful
Work as a team
Be responsible and kind
Do your best
Listen to others
Be a role model
Share

CHAPTER 12

Resource list and recommended reading

TEACHER: How many books have
you read in your lifetime?
PUPIL: I don't know. I'm not dead yet.

You Can Heal Your Life
by Louise L. Hay

Heal Your Body
by Louise Hay

Miracles Now: 108 Life-Changing Tools for Less Stress,
More Flow, and Finding Your True Purpose
by Gabrielle Bernstein

Mindfulness for Beginners: Reclaiming the Present
Moment--and Your Life
by Jon Kabat-Zinn

The Hidden Messages in Water
by Masaru Emoto and David A. Thayne

The Life-Changing Magic of Tidying: A simple, effective
way to banish clutter forever
by Marie Kondo

Speedcleaning: Room by room cleaning in the fast lane
by Shannon Lush and Jennifer Fleming

The 5 Love Languages of Children
by Gary D Chapman and Ross Campbell

The Five Love Languages of Teenagers: The Secret to
Loving Teens Effectively
by Gary D Chapman

The 5 Love Languages: The Secret to Love that Lasts
by Gary D Chapman

EFT TAPPING (The Tapping Solution) EFT Tapping For
Kids With Chronic Illness: Helping a Child With Chronic
Illness...
by Deborah D Miller

Your Fingertips: Learn EFT Tapping and Bring Miracles
with Your Fingertips!
by Benny Zhang

<u>My Private Parts are Private! A Guide for Teaching Children about Safe Touching</u>
by Robert Edelman and Selena Carter

<u>Saving Our Children from our Chaotic World: Teaching Children the Magic of Silence and Stillness.</u>
By Maggie Dent

Printed in the United States
By Bookmasters